ANNUAL
2001
The
Archers

The Archers has been part of my life since childhood.
Dum di dum di dum di dum was one of the earliest tunes I ever knew
– even though it meant it was bedtime!

Today *The Archers* is a passion for me as for so many. I am delighted
to be asked to provide a foreword for the *Archers Annual 2001* as it
gives me the chance to congratulate everyone on a wonderful year.
The characters have surprised, delighted and, at times, infuriated us
as they always do. The storylines have kept faith with the traditional
values of the programme whilst reflecting the often harsh realities of
farming in the modern world, from Tommy's action over the GM
crop trials to the eviction of the Grundys from Grange Farm and
their poignant struggle to make a life away from Ambridge.

The Archers is a precious part of Radio 4 and I wish it a very happy
50th birthday. I am looking forward to another gripping year.

Helen Boaden,
Controller, BBC Radio 4

contents

WHEN SHE LEAVES THE ROOM THERE'S THIS MARVELLOUS SENSE OF PEACE AND TRANQUILLITY

Lynda Snell FENG SHUI CONSULTANT

The Ambridge Album
1951–2001

FIFTY YEARS OF AMBRIDGE LIFE IN WORDS AND PICTURES

1951 Businessman George Fairbrother buys a farm and moves in with daughter Grace. Helen Carey and her son Alan visit Squire Lawson-Hope.

1952 Celebrity Gilbert Harding opens village fete. George marries Helen. Grace puts up the money for the riding school she starts with Christine Archer.

1953 John Tregorran arrives in Ambridge in a gypsy caravan. Tom Forrest has to evacuate his cottage after a fire breaks out in Squire Lawson-Hope's wood.

1954 Clive Lawson-Hope, the Squire's nephew, proposes to Christine but is rejected and leaves for Africa. Disappointment for John Tregorran, too, as Carol Grey turns him down.

1955 Phil marries Grace but in September she perishes in a stable fire at Grey Gables – Ambridge is stunned. Dan and Doris Archer buy Brookfield Farm.

1956 Foot and mouth disease strikes Brookfield – all Dan's sheep, pigs and cattle are slaughtered. Christine marries horse owner Paul Johnson.

1957 Jazz maestro Humphrey Lyttelton opens the village fete. Phil marries Jill Patterson. 'Aunt' Laura Archer arrives from New Zealand to start a new life in Ambridge.

1958 Most of Dan's crop is destroyed when fire breaks out in his Dutch barn. Jill produces twins – Shula and Kenton Archer.

Fact and fiction: the reality of the rehearsal room sees the cast gathered with scripts as *Archers* producer Tony Shryane (left) conducts rehearsals at the old BBC studios in Birmingham in 1955

Front (left to right): Joy Davies (Mrs Fairbrother); Anne Cullen (Carol Grey); Leslie Saweard (Christine Archer); Gwen Berryman (Doris Archer); Leslie Dunn (Paul Johnson).
Back: Leslie Bowmar (Mr Fairbrother); Norman Painting (Phil Archer); Harry Oakes (Dan Archer); Denis Folwell (Jack Archer)

The Archers as the public imagined them, gathered for tea and reading copies of the *Borchester Echo* in 1958

Those faces ring a bell –
Tom, Walter and Dan
practising at church in 1959

Tom Forrest (Bob Arnold) and Nigel Burton (Bryan
Kendrick) attired in their best suits for a chat with Sixties
film star Richard Todd, in Ambridge to open the village fete.
His visit coincided with the 3,000th episode in June 1962

In 1960 Charles Grenville
(Michael Shaw) and Carol
Grey (Anne Cullen)
celebrated their engagement
with a formal candlelit dinner

And what a difference a
few years makes –
a casually dressed Roger
Travers-Macy (Jeremy
Mason) takes a much
more relaxed approach
to his courtship of
Monica Downes (Jane
Rossington) in 1967

1959 Peggy and Jack
Archer buy The Bull with
£4,000 from Aunt Laura.
David Archer born and
nicknamed Snowball
because of his blond hair.

1960 Mrs Turvey
complains about Walter
Gabriel's pigs in Parson's
Field and he gets rid of
them. April Cottage and
Keeper's cottage are built.

1961 Dan forms Ambridge
Dairy Farmers with Fred
Barratt and Jess Allard.
Walter's junkyard, El
Dorado, opens in
Felpersham.

1962 Actor Richard Todd
opens the village fete. Phil
buys Allard's Farm,
renames it Hollowtree and
joins Ambridge Dairy
Farmers. Bob Dancer puts
a firework under a
pensioner on Bonfire
Night. Later his bike is
'mysteriously' found on fire.

1963 John's wife, Janet, is
killed in the same car crash
that badly injures Charles
Grenville. Sid Perks,
released from approved
school, becomes Jack
Woolley's chauffeur.

1964 Walter plays Long
John Silver with a real
parrot in the vicar's
production of Treasure
Island. Ralph Bellamy's
father Admiral Bellamy
dies.

1965 Charles dies, leaving
Manor House to his
widow, Carol. Jack Woolley
and Ralph Bellamy buy
the Grenville Estate.

1966 Scandal! Jennifer
Archer gets pregnant and
refuses to name the father.
Jethro Larkin gets a job at
the Berrow Estate and
brings his wife Lizzie and
daughter Clarrie back to
Ambridge. Polly Mead
weds Sid Perks.

1967 Jennifer gives birth to
a boy, Adam, and admits to
Lilian that the father is
cowman Paddy Redmond.
John Tregorran finally
marries Carol. Elizabeth
Ann Archer born.

1968 Nelson Gabriel is tracked down by Interpol, tried at Gloucester Assizes for a mail van robbery and found not guilty. Roger Travers-Macy marries Jennifer.

1969 Lilian marries 'Nick' Nicholson but a year later he's dead. Tony Archer takes a shine to vicar's daughter Tessa Latimer.

1970 Joe Grundy's dairy herd and his sons contract brucellosis.

1971 Lilian marries Ralph Bellamy, the 'Squire' of Ambridge. Tony gives her away as father Jack is in a clinic in Scotland.

1972 Martha marries woodman Joby Woodford. Walter proposes to Mrs P and she turns him down. Jack Archer dies in the clinic.

1973 Tony goes into partnership with Haydn Evans at Willow Farm. George Barford goes to work as Grey Gables' keeper. Joe is diagnosed with farmers' lung.

1974 Tony proposes to Mary Weston, but later the engagement is broken. By December he's marrying Haydn Evans' niece from Wales, Pat Lewis. Jack and Valerie Woolley divorce.

1975 Brian Aldridge buys 1,500 acres and Home Farm and has the house converted for him to live in.

1976 Carol is accused of shoplifting but is acquitted at Crown Court. Brian marries Jennifer. Jill collapses with myxoedema, a thyroid deficiency.

1977 Kate Aldridge is christened. Walter stays at Brookfield while the roof of Honeysuckle Cottage is replaced, and he ruins Doris's non-stick saucepans. Mike Tucker lights the Jubilee Beacon.

In 1958, the Hood family ran a bakery business in Ambridge.
Left to right: Roger Hood (Brian Roper); Percy (Ronald Baddiley); Joan (Nora Blair); Margaret (Jean Lester); Betty (Dorothy Smith); Diana (Eileen Barry)

Carol Grey (Anne Cullen) and first husband Charles Grenville (Michael Shaw) in 1961

Change partners – here's Carol in 1968 this time with new husband John Tregorran (Philip Morant) and (left) Jack Woolley (Philip Garston-Jones)

Tom and Pru Forrest (Bob Arnold and Mary Dalley) in 1968

Dan Archer (Edgar Harrison)
and Tom (Bob Arnold) in 1975

Another year, another village fete in 1975

Dan (Edgar Harrison, right)
and Walter Gabriel (Chriss
Gittins) get to grips with
the latest woolly additions
to the cast

1978 Christine's first
husband, Paul, dies. Shula
is breathalised and banned
from driving for a year.

1979 Christine marries
George and members of the
Hollerton Silver Band form
an archway of bugles
outside the church. A
daughter, Helen Archer, for
Pat and Tony, but she is
born with a dislocated hip.

1980 A year before her
diamond wedding Doris is
found dead in her armchair
by her granddaughter
Shula.

1981 Eddie Grundy
marries Clarrie and makes
his own record, Lambs to
the Slaughter. Jennifer
and John are co-authors of
Ambridge – An English
Village Through The
Ages. Tommy is born to
Pat and Tony.

1982 Sid's wife Polly 'Poll
Doll' is killed in a car
crash. Mark Hebden
advises Sid he can hold the
pub's licence alone.

1983 Eddie is banned
from The Bull for being
sick in the piano. David
buys a red Spitfire and falls
for Sophie Barlow, a
fashion designer.

1984 HRH Princess
Margaret spends the night
at Grey Gables en route to
an appointment. Neil
Carter marries pregnant
Susan Horrobin. Jack
Woolley falls off the
conservatory roof while
attempting to rescue his dog
Captain.

1985 First organic crops
harvested at Bridge Farm.
'Aunt' Laura dies without
signing her will, leaving her
lodger Colonel 'Freddie'
Danby homeless. Mark
Hebden marries Shula
(pictures by Lichfield).

1986 Dan dies. Mike is
bankrupt. Nelson gets a
shock when daughter
Rosemary turns up – he
had no idea he was a
father.

1987 Jethro suffers a fatal haemorrhage after an accident while trimming a tree. Agricultural student Ruth Pritchard is his replacement. Teacher Kathy Holland becomes the second Mrs Perks.

1988 Phil and Jill make David a partner in the farm and David makes Ruth Mrs David Archer.

1989 Terry Wogan plays golf at Grey Gables and Dame Judi Dench plays Pru – unheard for years until then. A BSE-afflicted cow knocks Brian over and he suffers post-traumatic epilepsy.

1990 Scottish rogue Cameron Fraser buys the Berrow Estate and has limited success wooing Caroline Bone. Kathy Perks renews her relationship with Detective Sergeant Dave Barry.

1991 Peggy marries Jack Woolley. Solicitor Usha Gupta goes into practice with Mark Hebden. DJ John Peel invites the Grundys to Radio One's Christmas lunch at Grey Gables.

1992 Reluctant father-to-be Cameron Fraser leaves pregnant Elizabeth at a motorway service station. She has an abortion.

1993 Celebrity Anneka Rice helps Lynda Snell refurbish the Village Hall. Pip Archer born. Clive Horrobin is a wanted man after an armed raid on the Village Shop. Susan shields him and is sent to prison for seeking to pervert the course of justice.

1994 Shula, distraught over husband Mark Hebden's tragic death in a car crash, finds she is pregnant and gives birth to Daniel in November. Elizabeth becomes Mrs Nigel Pargetter.

Gwen Berryman as
Doris Archer in 1978

Pru Forrest (Judi Dench) and Terry Wogan run through their lines for guest appearances in the 10,000th edition in 1989 with Jack Woolley (Arnold Peters)

1988 Ruth (Felicity Finch) and David (Timothy Bentinck) work together on the farm

Brian Aldridge (Charles Collingwood, **centre**) taking an interest in the Brookfield herd in 1983, though he had other things on his mind, namely the start of an affair with Caroline Bone

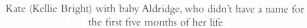

Kate (Kellie Bright) with baby Aldridge, who didn't have a name for the first five months of her life

In 1993 TV action woman Anneka Rice faced her biggest challenge during an emergency mission to redecorate the Village Hall – Lynda Snell (Carole Boyd)

Pat (Patricia Gallimore) and Tony (Colin Skipp) in their farm shop

1995 Caroline marries the sixty-something Guy Pemberton and former fiance the Rev Robin Stokes leaves Ambridge a disappointed man. Usha is the victim of racist attacks – the gang includes Roy Tucker.

1996 Hollywood's Tom Cruise kisses Clarrie four times during filming at Lower Loxley! GP Richard Locke is investigated over the death of a patient. Guy dies, leaving Caroline a wealthy widow, though disagreeable son Simon inherits the land.

1997 Clive Horrobin is out of prison and attacks George Barford in Grey Gables Country Park, leaving him unconscious. Brian Aldridge helps set up Borchester Land business consortium. Borchester bypass widening protest led by Kate Aldridge.

1998 John Archer is killed in a tractor accident. Kate has daughter Phoebe in a tepee at the Glastonbury Festival but fights a paternity battle with Roy Tucker. Dr Locke leaves after an affair with Shula. After her brief spell as scarlet woman, Shula marries vet Alistair Lloyd.

1999 Tommy Archer trashes his uncle Brian's trial crop of genetically modified oil seed rape. Pat Archer succumbs to depression, the delayed effect of son John's death. Julia Pargetter writes a bodice ripper – Passion's Plaything.

2000 Bankrupt, the Grundys are evicted from Grange Farm and move into a flat in Borchester. Debbie Aldridge marries Simon Gerrard. Brookfield's arguments over inheritance are stilled by Ruth's breast cancer.

WAYNE FOLEY asks the listeners of Ambridge …
What would **YOU** do if you
won a **million pounds?**

Alistair Lloyd, vet

'I'd like to go on safari with Shula. Perhaps Jill wouldn't mind keeping an eye on Daniel for the odd month or two – or we could get a nanny of course. Maybe we'd settle out there and Shula could learn to ride an elephant. Make a change from horses. But if we were to stay in Ambridge – let's face it Jill would have a fit if we didn't, let alone Bunty and Reg – I'd build us a new house with a surgery attached, so that Shula can enjoy life without being constantly reminded of the past, and I can work at home. Plus an unlimited supply of beer and wine for me and chocolate for Shula.'

Betty Tucker, shopkeeper

'Oh I don't know if I could cope with a big win. Not after what happened to that "Spend, Spend, Spend" woman. I suppose I would like to do something to help Mike get the sight in his eye back. I read somewhere that there's an eye expert in America who can do wonders, but it costs the earth. But for meself, well if I could just the once, buy meself a really nice outfit, shoes, coat and handbag, without having to think about how much it cost. That would make me really happy.'

William Grundy, trainee gamekeeper

'I'd buy Grange Farm lock stock and barrel, freehold and all, so that we can all go back and live where we belong, with enough money behind us to keep it going. Then I'd set up a company to run me own shoot and force Brian Aldridge out of the market. Oh and I'd buy Grandad a new pipe so that I could throw that stinking old one into the bin when he wasn't looking.'

Usha Gupta, solicitor

'First of all I'd like to pay for my Auntie Satya to be able to travel and see all her relatives that she misses so much. She'd go first-class everywhere and be treated like the queen she is. Then I'd set up a trust fund to provide proper legal representation for those special cases that fall through the net and don't get the help they need. Too many people, especially immigrants, don't understand the law or know their rights.'

Nigel Pargetter, laird of Lower Loxley

'Oh I say, steady on. That sort of thing hasn't happened to me since Matron pulled my name out of the hat and I was allowed to sit next to her in chapel. Well there's no denying that a few of the readies would come in handy after all we've laid out at Lower Loxley in the past year, plus the double expense of the twins, God bless them. Then there's paying off any more debts Mummy might have piled up without telling me. And buying her a nice villa in Spain would improve our relationship, for a while.'

Lynda Snell, receptionist at Grey Gables

'I suppose I'd put Robert back into business for himself again. But my great secret ambition is to build my own theatre in the grounds of Ambridge Hall. Well if Sam Wanamaker can do it, so can I.
Then I could employ some really excellent, classically trained actors, and not have to put up with the amateur dross like I do now.
Of course they would all stay in the Hall and we'd have sumptuous post-show suppers.'

Jolene Rogers, the Lily of Layton Cross

'If I had all that money I could buy up a swish recording studio and make all my own CDs, couldn't I? Or I could stay in a five-star hotel in Marbella and laze by the pool all day drinking beer. Just imagine me in my best bikini oiled up in the sun...'

Siobhan Hathaway, doctor's wife

'Like on the National Lottery you mean? Well we had the Sweepstake in Ireland for years and people got so worked up about it. I'm sure that I approve, really. It's just the thought of all those people who can ill-afford it having their hopes raised and then dashed again. Could I set up a public library in Ambridge? There's never been one as far as I know.'

Jean-Paul, master chef at Grey Gables

'First, I would have the greatest pleasure in telling Madame Woolley what exactly she could do with her boiled beef and carrots, plum duff, bread and butter pudding, and all the other boring English dishes she tries to force on to the Grey Gables menu. Then having upset the apple wagon, I would find a place to set up my own restaurant where good French cooking is really appreciated, and where they have never even heard of Grey Gables. My friend, he is recommending Stirchley. Do you know of such a place?'

Hayley Jordan, nanny

'I've often thought about this. When I see all those poor kids on the television in Kosovo and places like that, with no one to look after them. I could buy up a big house, like Arkwright Hall, or perhaps even go abroad and set up a home for them — a place where the children could be properly looked after by nurses and doctors and have enough to eat.'

Clarrie Grundy, barmaid and yoghurt maker

'It's a bit late for that now in't it? We could have done with a lottery win last year. I always said though that if I won a million I'd buy Eddie and me a little place in France in the country. Oh it was really lovely there. A bit old-fashioned, using horses and all that, but it was so peaceful, like I've always wanted life to be.'

© BBC Radio Borsetshire

BBC RADIO BORSETSHIRE FM **87.3**
THE WAYNE FOLEY BREAKFAST SHOW

BORCHESTER HOTSPOTS

YOUR GUIDE TO WHAT AMBRIDGE FOLK HAVE BEEN UP TO THIS YEAR IN THE COUNTY TOWN OF BORCHESTER

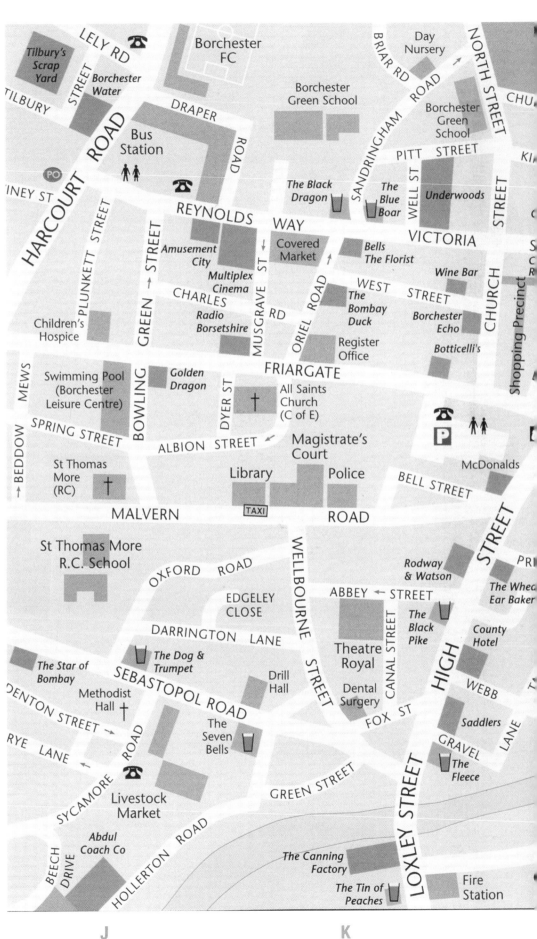

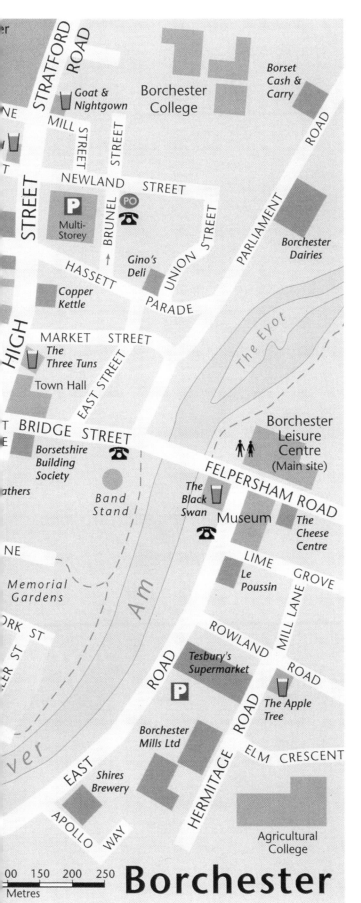

M9 Sin Gym at Borchester Leisure Centre

Sid and Jolene's hideaway. Working out paid off in a big way for Sid: he lost weight and gained the adoration of the Lily of Layton Cross when their eyes met across the chest expanders. Now she's pulling pints alongside him at The Bull, he has the benefit of her 36DD figure on a regular basis. If Sid had foreseen the result of the encounter, would he have kept his mind on his bench presses?

J11 10 Meadow Rise, off Sebastopol Road

'Not much of a meadow about it,' said Joe when the Grundys were re-housed in this council flat. Young Edward rebelled at being forced to share a room with his snoring Grandad, while neighbours complained to the council that they were illegally keeping ferrets in the flat. Poor Joe was like a fish out of water and his decline made Eddie determined to get the family back to Ambridge.

J9 BBC Radio Borsetshire

Brenda Tucker is serving her apprenticeship here, working regularly with presenter and local celebrity Wayne Foley.

J8 Ambridge Organics

Once a video shop, now Pat and Tony's latest venture into sales of organic food. Expensive wooden fittings and concealed lighting give it a modern 21st-century look, rather than a rustic, beard-and-sandals style. But is Helen the right choice as manager?

M10 The Cheese Centre – Felpersham Road

Stockist of Anne Baxter's high quality cheeses. Helen worked for Anne on her placement and was given good references and the promise of a job, which didn't interest her. Why be someone's lackey when you can rule the roost?

K11 The Canning Factory

Sir Sidney Goodman is a self-made man and his factory has provided local jobs for decades. Not renowned for his enlightened approach to labour relations (he ensured Usha Gupta lost a lucrative client when she had the temerity to act for his workers), Sir Sidney and his Spanish wife Mercedes have long presided over Borsetshire society and are cronies of Jack Woolley. Wisely, Eddie did not apply to him for a job.

K9 Borchester Register Office

Where the hatched, matched and despatched get entered in the book. It was here that Debbie became Mrs Simon Gerrard. A lovely day, but where was Brian? Alice was the ring-bearer, watched by Jennifer and Phoebe. No bridesmaids and no white Rolls-Royce, but Tony at the wheel of a decorated farm tractor and trailer conveyed the happy couple to the Grey Gables reception.

K9 Hurry That Curry (attached to Bombay Duck)

Eddie's short-lived evening job delivering Indian curry on the back of a moped was based here. Simon and Debbie were not pleased by his special delivery.

L9 (off map) Building Site

Location of Eddie's brief spell as a digger-driver. He's got the repartee to be a builder, but does he have the cleavage? The regular money helped for a while but all work and no Shires make Eddie short-tempered and he didn't enjoy the close supervision of a sarcastic foreman.

K8 Borchester Green School

When the Grundys lived in Borchester, Edward could walk to school, but the atmosphere at Meadow Rise made him restless and unhappy. At least on the school bus he could keep up with the gossip and eye up the girls at the same time.

J10 St Thomas More Roman Catholic Church

There is no Roman Catholic Church in Ambridge, so doctor's wife Siobhan Hathaway has to make regular pilgrimages into Borchester to worship at St Thomas More. She was there to attend the Good Friday vigil.

fact file

NAME: SUSAN CARTER née HORROBIN
BORN: 10 October 1963
ADDRESS: No 1 The Green, Ambridge.
FAMILY: Married to Neil. One daughter, Emma (born 1984) and one son, Christopher (born 1988)
OCCUPATION: Doctor's receptionist, assistant in the village shop, freelance literary typist
HOBBIES: Knitting, Women's Institute, becoming upwardly mobile
PAST SINS: Served prison sentence for sheltering brother Clive after armed raid on village shop; nagging

Highs

1983 Wins Pinky the pig at village fete, Neil builds it a shelter and love blossoms.
1983 Romantic weekend in London with Neil. She's pregnant and he wants to marry her. Phew!
1991 Her boss Cameron Fraser encourages her to learn computer skills – she's on her way up.
1999 She types up Julia Pargetter's raunchy novel and knits a beautiful baby shawl which Julia passes off as her own work.

Lows

1984 Daughter Emma born prematurely and develops jaundice.
1988 Gives birth to Christopher and blames herself for his hare-lip and cleft palette. Susan is revolted by the sight of him.
1993 Sentenced to six months for seeking to pervert the course of public justice. Neil gets involved with lonely farmer's wife Maureen Travis.
1994 Susan's white-collar hopes for Neil are shattered when he loses his job at Borchester Mills.

What if...
Susan had liked pigs a bit more?

Charlotte Martin

Charlotte was born at Fontainebleau near Paris, where her father was working at NATO headquarters, but she grew up in Solihull. She went to the Birmingham Theatre School and her first professional role was in *The Importance of Being Earnest* at Birmingham Rep. She has subsequently performed in the two-hander *Alba* for the Midlands Arts Centre and in *The Ambridge Pageant* tour of 1990.

Her TV credits include *The History Man, Howard's Way* and *A Very Peculiar Practice*. She was in a video for the group UB40 and had a part in the film *I Bought a Vampire Motorcycle*. Radio work includes numerous Afternoon Theatre and Saturday Night Theatre productions for Radio 4.

Charlotte lives in Birmingham with her husband and two daughters. She has worked as a choreographer and as a dance teacher but also enjoys writing short stories and poetry. In 1999, she graduated from the University of Birmingham with a BSc in Psychology.

Pigs have loomed large in Susan Carter's life, much to the dismay of this social-climbing mother-of-two. Her husband Neil adores rearing them – and it was a pig, after all, that brought the couple together – but for Susan, porkers symbolise everything she is trying to escape: the smells, the dirt, the vulgarity of life as an impoverished farming family.

Poor Susan. It always seems that just when her hopes are about to be realised they are cruelly dashed to the ground yet again. In the years since her husband Neil lost his job as a sales rep for the animal feeds firm Borchester Mills, the Carters have lived a hand-to-mouth existence.

Susan has struggled on, bringing in a little money from her part-time jobs, while Neil gets work wherever he can. In the strawberry season he works his smallholding in partnership with Mike Tucker, but most of the time it's casual employment to supplement what he enjoys most and Susan hates – working with his own outdoor breeding herd of pigs.

When Phil Archer offered Neil a job looking after an expanded pig operation at Brookfield, Susan was against it, even though Neil would be happy and would work regular hours for a fixed wage. But before the Carters could enjoy their good luck the Archers decided to abandon the project as part of streamlining at Brookfield. It was left to David Archer to break the news that Neil was no longer wanted. A furious Susan remarked: 'I don't know why you stand for it. They just treat you like a doormat'. And there may be some truth in that.

You can't blame Susan for trying to escape from her upbringing as a Horrobin. The Horrobins have long had a reputation in Ambridge as no-hopers and trouble-makers. So when she became involved with young, bright farmhand Neil Carter she felt all her troubles were over. Even when she became pregnant by him he did the decent thing and married her.

The trouble is Susan's aspirations have always far exceeded those of Neil. She hated it when he came home smelling of the pigsty and it was at her insistence that he applied for the white-collar job at Borchester Mills. He loathed the suit and briefcase life but Susan was in her element, particularly when she began to get work that lifted her, just a little, up the social ladder.

She came tumbling down, however, when her brother Clive, imprisoned for his part in an armed raid on the Village Shop, escaped and forced Susan to hide him from the police. The rest is history – a prison sentence, and disgrace as the sister of a jail-bird. She almost lost Neil, too, into the arms of Maureen Travis, who was quick to seize the opportunity of Susan's temporary absence.

When Neil resigned from Borchester Mills on a point of principle, he was relieved to return to farming. Susan was devastated and has found it hard to come to terms with the fact that she will always have to share her husband with his pigs.

BREAK-UP OF BROOKFIELD?

The inheritance row has divided the Archer family

THE BACKGROUND

The time has come for Phil Archer to take a lesser role in the running of Brookfield Farm, leaving David and Ruth, who are already partners, in control. Recent events have shown that, with their growing family, David and Ruth need the sizeable farmhouse as their home. Phil and Jill on the other hand would like to spend their retirement somewhere a bit smaller and easier to run.

However Brookfield Farm is the Archer family's inheritance, to be handed down for the benefit of future generations. If the farm is made over to David and Ruth there are implications for Kenton, Shula and Elizabeth, and their children. Phil and Jill considered the problem from every angle before finally seeking the advice of their accountant.

THE PROPOSAL

Their accountant proposed that Phil and Jill move out of Brookfield and buy a new home for around £200,000, handing over the farm to David and Ruth. To raise the necessary capital he recommended they sold a part of the Brookfield land to the young couple at 75 per cent of the market value. In addition Phil and Jill would require an annual pension to enable them to enjoy their retirement. After their parents died Shula and Elizabeth would each get half of the value of the new house. Kenton was not a cause for concern because he had been given his inheritance in advance some years previously – to help him out of yet another of his financial scrapes.

A FAREWELL TO PIGS

It's not just the end of pig production at Hollowtree, it's the end of an era. A large part of Phil's life has revolved around pigs. Even his engagement to Grace Fairbrother was dependent on him earning enough money from pig-breeding to marry her. Phil was heartbroken, but the pigs had to go because, as he reluctantly explains:

'The high pound is sucking in pig meat imports from everywhere and has ruined the UK pig industry.

'In addition, Britain has outlawed the stall-and-tether system for sows, so production costs are higher. But the UK imports pig meat from countries where the stall-and-tether system is still allowed.

'And because of BSE, UK pig farmers are not allowed to use meat-and-bone meal in their rations, though other countries can. This adds £5 per pig to UK production costs, as more expensive protein sources have to be used. In Switzerland, imported pig meat produced to a lower standard than Swiss meat has to carry a warning label saying so. Not the case in Britain.'

THE REALITY

If the proposal came into effect David and Ruth would have to find £35,000 a year out of the business before making any profit, £18,000 for Phil and Jill's pension, plus around £17,000 for the interest charges on the loan for the land purchase. In real terms Brookfield would belong to David and his heirs, cutting out his brother and sisters.

THE RESPONSE

DAVID AND RUTH: You're talking about £35,000 a year going out of the farm, before we can begin to pay ourselves!

SHULA: Goodness knows David and Ruth have worked hard enough for it. And thanks for thinking of me too.

KENTON: I know I've had my share of the capital already but what about the future profits?

ELIZABETH: ...So it all goes to David and Ruth. That's just not fair. I didn't know I had to get up and do the milking to get my share of the birthright!

IN CONVERSATION WITH ELIZABETH

You're obviously upset.

ELIZABETH: Of course I'm upset, wouldn't you be? Kenton's already had his inheritance and Shula's got Glebe Cottage. If David has Brookfield there's precious little left for me. I know I'll get half of Mum and Dad's retirement home but that doesn't compare with the whole of Brookfield Farm. My accountant says it must be worth at least one and a half million.

You have a beautiful home here. Do you really need more money?

Everyone seems to think I'm being greedy and that I've got more than enough with Lower Loxley. No-one seems to realise that we've sunk all our capital into the business or that what we're doing might not work! Nigel keeps telling me not to worry and we'll be fine but that just isn't the point. It's a matter of fairness. When all's said and done, why shouldn't the twins have the same inheritance as David and Ruth's children, Pip and Josh?

Your family seems to be torn to pieces over this issue. Is there no way you can compromise?

I've come up with a perfectly sensible scheme. I can share in the profits of Brookfield as a sleeping partner. I wouldn't expect to take anything out of the business at the moment, only if it becomes profitable in the future. At least that way I'll have some protection and so will the twins. Quite apart from anything else Pip and Josh will get something from Ruth's parents as well – we've only got Julia, and she's more of a liability.

Nigel tries to pacify Lizzie *Shula blames Lizzie but Alistair stays out of it*

How do your brother and sister feel about it?

Kenton's behind me one hundred per cent – but Shula's on Mum and Dad's side. But then she can afford to be, can't she?

And what about your heart condition? This can't be doing you much good.

You're quite right. If this keeps up I'll wind up back in hospital in no time!

Nigel, her husband, pacifies

NIGEL: I think it's all got a bit out of hand. I tell Lizzie she really shouldn't worry, the business is running quite well. And I don't think she should get so wound up. She's got her health to think of, and the twins, as well as all our plans for Lower Loxley.

ELIZABETH: Oh, Nigel!

NIGEL: You know I'm right, Lizzie. As long as we have each other, we'll be all right – everything else will fall into place given time.

Julia, her mother-in-law, antagonises

JULIA: I simply cannot understand why Elizabeth is so keen on Brookfield when she has a wonderful home like Lower Loxley. Many young women would love to be in her position and I think she's gone quite mad.

NIGEL: Mummy!

JULIA: I'm only saying what everyone else is thinking, Nigel.

Kenton agrees with Elizabeth

KENTON: It's just not on. I know that David and Ruth have worked their socks off but this is too big a reward. Brookfield belongs to all of us and we should all have our share.

Shula, her sister, is upset for her parents

SHULA: As far as I'm concerned it's up to Mum and Dad. I can't believe how badly Elizabeth and Kenton have behaved. I'd no idea that they could be so greedy and so hurtful. It's getting to the point when it looks as if they can't wait for Mum and Dad to die!

Alistair, Shula's husband, sits on the fence

ALISTAIR: I'm just amazed at the way Shula and Kenton have argued and shouted at each other down the phone. Twins are supposed to be close aren't they?

IN CONVERSATION WITH DAVID AND RUTH

How are you going to make it work?

DAVID: To be honest I'm not sure. In general terms we're just going to have to rationalise the business, cut costs wherever possible, simplify management, and cut staff. We've talked it all over with a consultant who suggested that we should get rid of the sheep and concentrate on milk and cereals. But it looks as if we'll have to lose Bert Fry as well as Neil Carter, and I can't imagine what that will mean to him and Freda. It will break his heart.

And what about Elizabeth?

Now that's a good question. I've taken all the costings over to Lower Loxley to show her exactly what the financial position would be and how untenable it would be for her to have shares in the farm. But I just can't get through to her. It's like she's on a different planet.

Ruth, do you feel sympathetic towards your sister-in-law?

RUTH: You must be joking! There's Elizabeth, living in a stately home with a fairly secure background and two beautiful babies. What more does she need?

I understand that you are still recovering from breast cancer. Do you think the strain you've been under has had anything to do with it?

Well it certainly hasn't helped. Nothing's turned out the way I wanted it to. David and I had just started thinking about another baby but that's out of the question at the moment of course. And we can't do anything until all this is resolved.

Is there really no way you can compromise, David?

DAVID: I worked out another offer with our accountant and took that to Elizabeth. I said if we ever give up the farm, she can have a share in the proceeds of the sale. But she rejected that. She says we're not offering her anything in real terms because we'll never sell up. I don't know. All I'm trying to do is find a workable solution to an impossible situation! But I'm obviously wasting my time.

IN CONVERSATION WITH PHIL AND JILL

Did you ever think that your retirement plans would bring about such upset in the family?

PHIL: Certainly not. Jill and I thought about it for some time before tackling our accountant. We thought our plan was fair, although it would be hard for David and Ruth to find enough money from the business to buy us a house and pay us an annual pension.

JILL: Phil and I never expected Elizabeth to react as she did. David and Ruth are partners with us and have worked very hard for the farm. It's our family business which we wanted to hand down to future generations. We had no intention of hurting Elizabeth's feelings but if we try to please everybody we'll have to split up the farm.

What about the plan for rationalisation David and Ruth have put forward?

PHIL: I was very reluctant but David was adamant. I'm particularly upset about losing the pigs and letting down Neil. David tells me that I'm living in the past and that there's neither money nor security in pigs these days but I find it very difficult to accept.

JILL: Whichever way we turn we wind up doing the wrong thing. Phil says Elizabeth is just going to have to accept our plan as it stands. There seems to be no reasoning with her and we know that David has genuinely tried to work out a scheme to satisfy her.

In any case you've had other things to think about

PHIL: We certainly have. I've had to keep an eye on Jill I can tell you. We knew Elizabeth was going to have an operation on her heart but Ruth took us completely by surprise.

JILL: I can still remember how mortified I was when she told us, because I'd jumped to completely the wrong conclusion – I thought she was pregnant. And she was in hospital very quickly after that, and then into chemotherapy. She's still not fully out of the woods yet but we are very hopeful.

And the inheritance struggle?

JILL: Oh we're not thinking about that at the moment, are we Phil? Something like this puts everything into perspective. We'll sort something out in the end I'm sure, and in the meantime it will just have to wait.

GOODBYE NEIL AND BERT?

With no pigs to look after Neil Carter had to be told there wasn't a job for him after all. He took it hard, although he understood that the Archers had no choice in the matter.

Next to go at Brookfield could be farmhand Bert Fry. David and Ruth will do their best to keep him on without cutting his hours too much. They are fighting to stay afloat now and Bert's survival on the farm hangs in the balance.

Ruth's darkest hour

When her character, Ruth Archer, developed breast cancer, Felicity Finch turned to real-life sufferers to help her portray the anxiety and distress of the killer disease

Ruth Archer, wife of David Archer and mother of Pip, seven, and three-year-old Josh, discovered a lump in her breast a few weeks before her 32nd birthday. It turned out to be a malignant tumour and she had to have her breast removed, followed by a course of chemotherapy.

For an actor, such a sombre storyline demands sensitivity combined with a cool appreciation of the medical facts, explains Felicity Finch.

'When I heard that Ruth was to have breast cancer I was overwhelmed by the huge challenge. I knew there would be listeners with breast cancer, and others knowing someone with the disease.

'I read everything relevant, including the *Breakthrough Cancer Handbook*, which covers diagnosis to operation, the after care, and several case histories. I listened to an American radio programme where people talk about their cancers. I was also moved by a book by journalist Ruth Picardie, *Before I Say Goodbye*, which is made up mainly of newspaper columns she wrote in the months leading up to her death from breast cancer. These are my props which I refer to when I receive a new batch of scripts.

'I also spoke to two women who previously had breast cancer, and before recording I checked on how they reacted at each stage of the disease.'

Working with Tim Bentinck, who plays David Archer, is great, she says. 'We know each other well, and he had the experience of worry when his children were ill as babies. Because Tim got a part in a film we had to record several episodes together over a short space of time, including the scenes when the oncologist says

> When I heard that Ruth was to have breast cancer I was overwhelmed by the huge challenge. I knew there would be listeners with breast cancer, and others knowing someone with the disease.

it's cancer, and later, when we tell Phil and Jill. It really flowed and everyone treated us with great sensitivity.'

To prepare for the mastectomy, Felicity had to consider how a woman used to being in complete control of her life and health would feel to wake up without a breast and with having to take advice from the oncologist and breast care nurse.

Back from hospital Ruth had to rest and not work. 'It's unbearable for such a physical person. She can't do much for Pip and Josh. Not having children myself it was difficult to react when Ruth feels she may die, and not be there for them. Undergoing the chemotherapy treatment and coping one day at a time produced feelings of mixed emotions.

'At the end of the day I'm an actor and I just get on with it. I draw on my 13 years being Ruth and hope that the reality of the scenes will work, but in the back of my mind are all those women who are suffering or who have suffered the trauma of the disease.'

RoguesGallery

In a departure from its usual Brit Art sensibilities, the new
Lower Loxley art gallery hosts a one-off show, recalling
Ambridge's bad boys and girls in a series of all-too-lifelike
portraits. Those who said Cameron Fraser and Simon
Pemberton should hang are about to get their wish…

MATT CRAWFORD

Mad, bad and dangerous to know

Hard-bitten boss of Borchester Land, mean Matt Crawford hasn't won any hearts in Ambridge. A businessman, he knows precious little about the countryside and villagers doubt he can tell one end of a cow from the other. Sadly, he thinks he's one for the ladies but he couldn't tempt Debbie Aldridge, who found his wide-boy charms about as appealing as foot-and-mouth.

He got his revenge though, by scuppering her plans for Grange Farm. Having relished evicting the Grundys, he took even greater delight in flogging it as a 'toy' farm – the farmhouse with a mere five acres attached – and absorbing the rest into Borchester Land.

The only positive thing you can say about Crawford is that he's a match for Brian Aldridge, outmanoeuvring him over the Grundy affair so that Brian wound up with the blame.

Brian's still smarting from that one. And 'Mad' Matt is still smiling.

SIMON PEMBERTON

The rich bully boy

Tall, dark, handsome, rich – Simon seemed perfect son-in-law material to most Ambridge matrons, who were more than ready to clasp him to their maternal bosoms. But the signs that all was not well beneath the cool, gentlemanly exterior were there from the start. Simon was rotten to his father, the distinguished Guy Pemberton, vile to the Grundys and a bit odd with his lady friends.

As landowner of Ambridge's Berrow Estate, Simon sprang to ignominy when he was named as the second worst landlord in the country by The Land is Ours Campaign. He was nominated for his mistreatment of the Grundys, and for his attempt to maximise cash profits from his estate at the expense of the land and his tenants. It didn't bother him much.

In love, he was equally self-seeking. He oiled his way into Shula Hebden's good graces by being kind to her small son Daniel, but had no compunction about two-timing her with an old flame. When she challenged him, he lashed out at her.

Shula kept quiet about what had happened, watching with some concern when he moved on to Debbie Aldridge. Simon courted Debbie zealously, but she grew increasingly unhappy at his treatment of the Grundys. When she realised she could never love a man like him, he lost control – and Debbie received a violent beating.

The whole miserable business came out in court when he had to plead guilty to assaulting her. He was ordered to pay costs and a small amount in compensation, but was given a conditional discharge. Shula, Debbie and the rest of Ambridge were aghast.

He quickly packed his elegant luggage and left for Dubai, much to the relief of the same matrons who had held such high hopes when he first arrived in Ambridge.

PADDY REDMOND

He done Jennifer wrong

In 1965, philanderer Paddy Redmond arrived in Ambridge to work for Dan Archer, full of Irish blarney. He captivated a few hearts, including that of the young Jennifer Archer, who succumbed to his charms only for him to return from holiday engaged to another woman. Two months later his fiancée, Nora McAuley, arrived from Belfast to work behind the bar at The Bull.

Paddy soon tired of domestic bliss and headed off, leaving behind a devastated Nora and a pregnant Jennifer. Fourteen years later in 1981, he dropped into The Bull searching for Nora. Looking prosperous, he was on his way to a farm manager's job in Ulster.

When Jennifer, now Mrs Brian Aldridge, saw him with Nora she panicked. She had never told Paddy about their son, Adam. It was left to Nora to spill the beans. Once Paddy knew, he telephoned Jennifer asking her to bring Adam to The Feathers so that they could meet.

Brian stopped Jennifer from going, went to meet Paddy himself and threatened legal action if he made any move to see Adam. With the luck of the Irish Paddy did bump into Jennifer and Adam by accident before he left, and so caught a glimpse of the son and wife he might have had.

DAVE BARRY

Not the laughing policeman

In the 1950s Ambridge had a succession of village bobbies, all brought up in the 'Evenin' all' school of *Dixon of Dock Green*. Then along came young Dave Barry. He wasn't a lowly constable, he was a detective sergeant, and he never let you forget it. He was also deeply unpopular.

In 1982 he arrested Nelson Gabriel on suspicion of handling stolen goods in his antiques shop, but had to release him owing to lack of evidence. Nelson couldn't resist a quiet smirk.

In the same way he was more than ready to charge Eddie Grundy with rustling cattle from Home Farm until lack of evidence forced him to drop that case too. 'Just you wait, Eddie Grundy,' Dave Barry often proclaimed. Eddie is still waiting.

Dave joined the Grey Gables Golf Club, and was drawn to play against the deputy chief constable in a tournament. When he lost, his caddie, who happened to be Eddie Grundy, enlivened the proceedings by suggesting that Dave had deliberately played badly to please the senior officer. No-one disagreed.

The entire village knew when Dave became involved with young teacher Kathy Holland. Their tempestuous relationship lasted for two years until Kathy decided to marry Sid Perks. Even then the unctuous Dave didn't give up, and offered rather more than tea and sympathy when Kathy's marriage went through a bad spell.

After Kathy finished their affair, Dave realised that he was going nowhere. Severe depression followed, and, having learned nothing from all his experiences in Ambridge he tried to cheer himself up by telling all to an amused Nelson Gabriel.

There were no tears in Ambridge when in 1990 DS Dave Barry decided that enough was enough and applied for a transfer to St Albans.

CAMERON FRASER

Cameron the Cruel

There is one name that will always be greeted with hostility wherever it's heard in Ambridge: Cameron Fraser.

This apparently gentle Scot was full of charm and sophistication when he arrived in 1990. He had bought the Berrow Estate and spent a great deal on renovating the Dower House as his home. The staff were all assured that their jobs were safe in his hands, and everything in the Cameron Fraser garden seemed rosy.

Rosy enough for Caroline Bone to fall for him – she was recovering from her fruitless affair with Dr Mathew Thorogood, and Cameron appeared to be the dashing, successful man of her dreams. In time, Caroline began to see through the façade, and when she made it known that she had finished with Cameron, Elizabeth Archer was ready and willing to take her place.

By then Cameron had managed to raise quite a few hackles in Ambridge. Peggy, now Mrs Woolley, was glad to end her job in the Estate Office; Shula clashed with him over his treatment of tenants; and when Mike Tucker lost an eye while working for the estate it was farm manager Geoff Williams whom Cameron held responsible for the accident.

Elizabeth was besotted with Cameron, but the crunch came when she told him that she was pregnant and wanted to have his baby. From his reaction to the news, it was clear that he did not share her desire.

By now the pleasant Fraser mask was slipping fast. His company in Scotland was on the verge of bankruptcy, and his many clients were asking what was happening to their money. Embezzlement was the name of his game and it hadn't paid off.

Cameron reassured Elizabeth by telling her that their future together needed careful planning and suggested they take a holiday. It was on the way to this holiday that poor, trusting, pregnant Elizabeth was unceremoniously left at a motorway service station. Like a bag of dirty laundry she was dumped, while Cameron sped away.

As the news spread, many people in Ambridge, including Caroline and Mrs Antrobus, revealed how much money they had invested in Cameron's schemes – money they were never to see again.

It's now nine years since he disappeared. Surely even he wouldn't be foolish enough to show his face in Ambridge again – would he?

fact file

NAME: REV JANET FISHER
BORN: 1960s
ADDRESS: The Vicarage, Darrington
OCCUPATION: Vicar of the Amvale Parishes
HOBBIES: Charity walks, cricket, amateur dramatics, keeping fit, Beating the Bounds
PAST SINS: Between Janet and her Maker

Highs

1994 Janet as vicar of Darrington wins her licence to preach in Ambridge, Penny Hassett and Edgeley as the four parishes merge.
1997 Plays Puck in Lynda Snell's open-air production of *A Midsummer Night's Dream* at Ambridge Hall.
1998 Gathers support for Millennium Wood, persuading the Aldridges to donate land.
1999 Sees bells cast at Whitechapel Foundry and organises consecration service for new bell 'Old Tom' in memory of Tom Forrest.
Completes charity walk to Cologne for Jubilee 2000, the campaign to persuade the West to wipe out debt in Third World countries.

Lows

1994 Opposition to her appointment as first woman vicar dismays her, though she plans to win the sceptics over.
1998 Appeals for return of the antique silver candlesticks stolen from St Stephen's.
1998 Has to eat two harvest suppers as she rushes from parish to parish. Leaves tell-tale fruit pie in pulpit at St Stephen's.

What if...
Janet forgot her vows?

If there is one thing the Rev Janet Fisher can be proud of it is that St Stephen's Parish Church has a refurbished peal of eight bells, blessed by the Bishop of Felpersham, and that they were ready in time to welcome in the Millennium. It says a great deal about Janet's understanding and charity that one of the new bells is inscribed to the memory of the late Tom Forrest and his wife, Pru. Tom, former church warden and captain of the bell tower, was the most vociferous opponent of Janet's appointment as the first female vicar of Ambridge.

Funds were raised, the bells were cast and the ceremony arranged in the same year that Janet made her successful sponsored walk to Cologne for Jubilee 2000, the campaign to wipe out Third World debt. Janet also led a mixed cricket team, nicknamed God's XI, against Ambridge, and played Puck in the Ambridge Players' *A Midsummer Night's Dream*.

Yet integration into Ambridge's tight little community was difficult at first. When the Rev Robin Stokes decided to leave Ambridge in 1996, the Bishop proposed that the Rev Janet Fisher, already vicar of Darrington, Edgeley and Penny Hassett, should also take over the parish of Ambridge.

Ambridge parishioners were aghast. They didn't want a combined benefice and they certainly didn't want a female vicar. Fierce debate took place at the Parochial Church Council, but in the end a dwindling congregation and mounting costs meant that they had to agree, however reluctantly, to the idea.

Nevertheless, many remained opposed to Janet's appointment and Tom Forrest felt so strongly that he, along with Peggy Woolley, went to worship elsewhere.

The turning point came when Martha Woodford died. Janet conducted the funeral service in a way that brought her closer to the villagers and they viewed her in a more kindly light. Eventually, even Tom re-joined the flock.

Janet is tireless in her work for the parish. She was a key fundraiser for the Millennium bells and redoubled her efforts when it was discovered that a new frame was needed to support them. A sponsored bike ride round the villages was a great success.

She encouraged the villagers to find the land and the money for an Ambridge Millennium Wood. She was devastated when a pair of antique silver candlesticks was stolen from St Stephen's (they were recovered), but resisted calls to lock the church.

And who else but Janet Fisher would agree to attend two harvest suppers on the same evening, rather than let down one of her parishes?

Ambridge has come to accept and be thankful for its first woman vicar. But will Rev Fisher be happy to remain in Borsetshire? Or will the Church decide to use her undoubted talents elsewhere?

Moir Leslie

Moir enjoys playing Ambridge's first woman vicar, though she originally joined the cast in 1985 as David Archer's fiancée, dress designer Sophie Barlow.

She has been heard in productions on BBC Radios 3, 4 and the BBC World Service, including several series of the comedy *Flying The Flag*. She was Beatrix Potter in *Exit Miss Potter*, Maggie in *Mill On The Floss* and played the title roles in Charlotte Bronte's *Shirley* and JM Barrie's *Mary Rose*.

Her theatre work includes West End productions of *For Services Rendered*, *Reflections* and *Troubadour* and several British and international tours. Moir has directed *Educating Rita* and *Relatively Speaking* for Richmond Productions, touring the Middle East, India and Pakistan. TV work includes *The Bill*, *Grafters*, and *Dalziel and Pascoe*.

Moir lives in London with her husband and teenage daughter.

Bert Fry's Gardening Tips

He's more of a Percy Thrower than a Charlie Dimmock but what Bert Fry doesn't know about gardening in Ambridge you could write on the back of a seed packet. He's sharing his seasonal tips, starting here with what to do in the garden in winter and spring.

winter

If you're thinking about turning over some soil that's not been cultivated before, don't wait until the frost has a hold – otherwise you're likely to break the handle of your spade or even your arm.

Then there's the question of what to add to the soil. For this you need to ask someone with a little local knowledge. What's good for Ambridge may not be right over Felpersham way. Don't ask in the garden centre or they'll try and sell you this, that and the other. A neighbour will know best and if luck's on your side he'll come and give you a hand.

There's nothing like a good bit of digging to warm you up on a cold day. Over at Woodbine Cottage there used to be a robin who would come down when I was digging. Looking for earthworms, he was. I'd put my spade in the ground and he'd perch on the handle and we'd look at each other for a while before he'd fly off.

'March winds and April's showers
Bring forth May's flowers'

Then there's those shrubs, fruit trees and roses from the nursery to get in. If the ground is too hard or too frosty they can be left in their wrappings for a few days as long as the roots have something moist around them. After a few days they can go into a shallow trench in a sheltered spot.

Keep an eye on the stakes supporting fruit trees. The supporting straps shouldn't be too tight or they'll cut into the bark. I use a pair of Freda's lyle stockings.

A spot of pruning and trimming – 'specially on that copper beech hedge – clear up the leaves and other debris and then it's time to go in for a nice cup of tea in front of the fire.

spring

My Freda always insists that I wear my thick coat when I get into the garden, as the weather can be treacherous in spring.

'Keep buttoned up to chin
Till May be in'

I was never quite sure whether that meant until the month of May is in or until the may tree is in blossom, which can be quite early. Best to make your own decision, I reckon. It's the same with the crop of early potatoes. I know some old gardeners who swear by putting them in on Good Friday.

I've already got my main crop put to sprout, nicely tucked up under the shelf in the potting shed. And I've got a few seed boxes going, with Brussels sprouts, cabbage and cauliflower.

Now go around where you dug out the seed beds last autumn, rake off the sticks, clear away dead leaves and break up large lumps of soil with the back of the rake. And pull out any weeds that have had the audacity to grow during the winter. Then rake it until the soil looks like crumbs, and it should be like that about an inch down. If you can't get your seed in right away cover it with some polythene.

Have you got a pile of manure ready for digging in a bit later? No-one in Borsetshire is too far away from a plentiful supply of manure, but do make sure it's well rotted, otherwise it will do more harm than good.

If you're quick you can still prune your rose bushes and clear out all the rubbish at the base. And keep an eye on your gooseberry bushes or the birds will be down picking out the buds. Those pesky blue tits are the worst. Nice to see them in the garden but they can do a lot of damage when they're hungry.

Read Bert's advice for summer and autumn on page 62

BRITAIN'S FARMERS WANT HELP NOT CROCODILE TEARS!

Borchester Echo Reporter

Ambridge villagers are up in arms about the eviction of the Grundy family from Grange Farm. A petition has been signed by hundreds of those who feel that, once again, the little man has been sacrificed upon the altar of commercial greed. It was presented to Borchester Land, the consortium that owns Grange Farm. The *Echo* decided to drop in for a pint of Shires at the local pub, The Bull, and we discovered feelings were running high.

'It's disgusting!' said receptionist Mrs Susan Carter, 36. 'British farmers are treated worse than car workers. The Grundys may not be the best farmers in the world but there's no call to get rid of them after all the years they've been at Grange Farm. And that Brian Aldridge is no better than he should be. You'd have thought he'd have put in a word to help them, but, oh no, he's got bigger fish to fry, hasn't he?'
(Editor's query: Do we have a quote from Mr Aldridge?
Reporter: Er, no. He was rather short when I called, typical nouveau riche type I suspect, swimming pool, Merc, real capitalist, no time for the huddled masses whose toil helps keep his wife in posh hats.
Editor: On the contrary. Mr Aldridge is a delightful man with whom I have had the pleasure of dining several times at our mutual friend Sir Sidney Goodman's house, together with Mr Woolley.)

Joe Grundy, 78, grandfather of the unfortunate family, said: 'I inherited the tenancy of Grange Farm from generations of Grundys. I feels I has let them down. But we've always bin dogged by misfortune. For some people everything they touches turns to gold. For us Grundys it's always turned to dung.'

Philip Archer, 72, owner of nearby Brookfield Farm, refused to comment.

Joe's son Eddie, 49, says he'll never get over the mortification of having his livelihood taken away and his family's personal possessions valued for auction.
(Editor: Did Mr Grundy really use the word 'mortification'? I understood he was a farm labourer.
Reporter: No sir, his actual words were 'I were gutted' but I felt mortification lent him a somewhat noble air, the individual confronting his destiny...
Editor: Oh for goodness sake, this isn't Hamlet.)

Eddie said: 'It's a terrible thing to see your home taken over by strangers. They showed no respect. There were tools there that my grandad cared for, and they chucked them about as if they was nothing.

'They called our old bits "rare and unusual farm implements". But nobody bought them to use them properly. They've taken away the old wooden hay rakes and gin traps, the carthorse collars and harnesses to decorate pubs, would you believe! And some TV ponces bought my boot-scraper and Clarrie's kettle. She reckons she'll see 'em on Heartbeat.'
(Editor: Hmm. Why haven't we got an interview with Mrs Grundy, the woman's angle, 'My tragedy, me and my children being made homeless, my beautiful home destroyed' etc.
Reporter: Mrs Grundy was too upset to comment, I'm afraid.
Editor: Really. Some people are so sensitive. Would she talk if we offered her a makeover, do you think?)

SAVE THE GRUNDYS PETITION

We the undersigned believe that the Grundy family should not be evicted from the home and land their family has rented for generations. We ask that Borchester Land reconsider and give the Grundys a fair chance to repay their debts.

David Archer
Ruth Archer
Jill Archer
Caroline Pemberton
Tommy Archer
Dolly Tredgold.
Clive Horrobin.
Sid Perks.
Jolene Rogers.
Neil Carter
Tracey Horrobin
Alf Grundy.
Susan Carter
Marjorie Antrobus
Hayley Jordan
Snatch Foster
Baggy

(Continued over)

LISTENERS FIGHT BACK!

When it became clear that the Grundys were really going to be evicted, the Archers office and the Archers Addicts headquarters were inundated with letters and e-mails all crying the same thing – 'Please oh please don't let the Grundys leave Ambridge!'

Fans' ideas for saving them ranged from Clarrie purchasing a winning lottery ticket to Caroline Pemberton bailing the family out. The Grundys were advised to dig for buried treasure or sell William into slavery. One brave person suggested that Eddie could be 'discovered' and earn a fortune from his singing…

LIFE AFTER GRANGE FARM...

Eddie Grundy – Hurry That Curry!

Town life wasn't what he was used to but Eddie did his best. His building site job was short-lived while his night job delivering curry ended abruptly when he had to deliver to Simon and Debbie Gerrard. Not only was Debbie the daughter of Brian Aldridge, whom Eddie blamed for the eviction, but he'd heard rumours that the couple were going to rent Grange Farm. It was too much! Enraged, Eddie hurled the curry on to the doorstep and zoomed off on his moped, only pausing to give away the rest of the curries he was supposed to deliver. He told the manager where to stuff his chappatis and returned to casual work on the farms.

Clarrie Grundy – This Ain't Ambridge

Clarrie hated living in a two-bedroom flat at Meadow Rise in Borchester. She wasn't used to the noise, the dirt or people encroaching on her space. She's had a hard time and will give anyone who needs it a bit of useful advice.

CLARRIE'S TOP TIPS

1. **Don't bin the bills**
2. **Don't listen to any of your husband's bright ideas**
3. **Or his father's**
4. **Pay your rent on time**
5. **Save something for a rainy day**
6. **Never trust an Aldridge**

Joe Grundy – Anyone At Home?

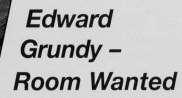

Flat life was not for Joe. He had nothing to do all day and no-one to talk to. The old folk's luncheon failed to tempt him and the local pubs couldn't begin to compare with The Bull. Matters came to a head when he went missing for two days and was found barely conscious in a ditch. Eddie promised that when Joe came out of hospital they would return to Ambridge. A promise that he kept – although in typical Grundy style!

William Grundy – Thanks Mrs Pemberton

In true Fairy Godmother style Caroline Pemberton whisked godson William away to rooms of his own at the Dower House. His adored Jersey heifer, Baby Spice, was safe at Brookfield and he even had his own television. The only fly in the ointment is his brother Edward.

Edward Grundy – Room Wanted

Edward (left) refused to sleep in the same room as his grandfather, preferring the settee. He found a soulmate in Jazzer and annoyed his brother by dropping in at the Dower House. And when his dad insisted that he couldn't stay on his own once the family went back to Ambridge, Edward decided he'd rather sleep in a 'bender' than in a caravan rocked by Joe's snoring.

The Grundys Are Back

Eddie kept his promise and the Grundys came back to Ambridge, even though at first it was in a caravan parked illegally on Estate land. 'We're back where we belong,' said Joe, breathing a deep sigh of contentment, as he looked out towards Lakey Hill. Well – almost.

THE END OF AN ERA FOR EDDIE

It's been a tough year for the Grundys. So tough that someone sent Trevor Harrison who plays Eddie a cheque for £5 to help him out. 'I haven't cashed it,' says Trevor. 'I'll hang on to it for Eddie.'

It's been a challenging year for the actors playing the Grundys, too. Trevor has mixed feelings. 'I loved the chance to play some wonderfully dramatic scenes and show a different side to Eddie – but some of that emotion was for real.

'Listeners told me they were sure that Eddie and Joe would pull through, like they've done in the past. They thought we'd find some treasure, or win the lottery, or that a third party would arrive and save us – perhaps Caroline.

'Of course the Grundys weren't saved and that really got to people. It brought home to them what all the changes in farming means to small farmers. From that point of view I thought it was an especially powerful story.

'It also had a knock-on effect on the development of the boys as characters. William is the sensible one of the family. He's becoming independent and shows no signs of following in his dad's footsteps. Edward used to be the good one with the voice of an angel but now he's become a chip off the old block, swigging back the beer and getting into trouble as a teenage tearaway, just like Eddie.

'I was surprised at how emotional I felt about Eddie leaving Grange Farm, and to tell the truth we all shed a tear when we recorded the episode in which we had to sell off the stock. The director very kindly brought in a bottle of wine and we sat outside the studio and carried on talking about the scene for ages. It's not like a job where you just take the money and go home afterwards. *The Archers* is a very special institution for the actors as well as everyone else.

'A couple of weeks after the Grundys left Grange Farm for good I went on a trip and as we drove past a couple of farms I suddenly thought to myself: Oh, I'm not in a farm any more!

'I've been a Grundy at Grange Farm pretending to milk cows for more than 21 years. It's the end of an era professionally as well as personally.'

Morwenna's Magic

Are you a noble elm or a loving apple? Check New Age guru Morwenna's birthday chart for your woodland birth sign, but turn the page to discover what tree warden George Barford makes of it all

Birth Dates	Tree	Key Quality	Characters
December 23 – January 1	Apple	loving	Debbie Aldridge
January 2 – January 11	Fir	mysterious	Pat Archer, Jennifer Aldridge
January 12 – January 24	Elm	noble	
January 25 – February 3	Cypress	faithful	Kathy Perks, Roy Tucker
February 4 – February 8	Poplar	uncertainty	
February 9 – February 18	Cedar	confidence	William Grundy, Tony Archer
February 19 – February 29	Pine	particular	Tommy Archer
March 1 – March 10	Weeping Willow	melancholy	
March 11 – March 20	Lime	reluctance	Eddie Grundy
March 21	Oak	strength	
March 22 – March 31	Hazelnut	extraordinary	
April 1 – April 10	Rowan	sensitivity	Caroline Pemberton, Robert Snell
April 11 – April 20	Maple	independence	Helen Archer
April 21 – April 30	Walnut	passion	Elizabeth Pargetter, Phil Archer
May 1 – May 14	Poplar	uncertainty	Clarrie Grundy
May 15 – May 24	Chestnut	honesty	Neil Carter
May 25 – June 3	Ash	ambition	Lynda Snell
June 4 – June 13	Hornbeam	good taste	Nigel Pargetter, Sid Perks
June 14 – June 23	Fig	sensibility	Ruth Archer
June 24	Birch	inspirational	
June 25 – July 4	Apple	loving	
July 5 – July 14	Fir	mysterious	
July 15 – July 25	Elm	noble	Jack Woolley
July 26 – August 4	Cypress	faithful	Betty Tucker,
August 5 – August 13	Poplar	uncertainty	Shula Hebden Lloyd, Kenton Archer
August 14 – August 23	Cedar	confidence	Julia Pargetter
August 24 – September 2	Pine	particular	
September 3 – September 12	Weeping Willow	melancholy	
September 13 – September 22	Lime	reluctance	Joe Grundy, David Archer
September 23	Olive	wisdom	
September 24 – October 3	Hazelnut	extraordinary	Kate Aldridge, Jill Archer
October 4 – October 13	Rowan	sensitivity	Susan Carter
October 14 – October 23	Maple	independence	Tom Forrest
October 24 – November 11	Walnut	passion	George Barford
November 12 – November 21	Chestnut	honesty	Peggy Woolley, Brian Aldridge
November 22 – December 1	Ash	ambition	Mike Tucker
December 2 – December 11	Hornbeam	good taste	
December 12 – December 21	Fig	sensibility	Christine Barford
December 22	Beech	creativity	

TREE WARDEN GEORGE BARFORD RECKONS MORWENNA KNOWS ABOUT AS MUCH ABOUT TREES AS HE DOES ABOUT LINE DANCING. SO HERE'S HIS OPINION OF WHO'S AN OAK OR AN ELDER...

APPLE

The common wild apple tree, known as Crab Apple, is found in untended woods. Bushy and tangled, its long shoots often stick out of the framework. The bright green leaves

BEECH

A graceful, attractive tree, sometimes called the Lady of the Woods, the Beech stands upright with a network of fine branches. The wood is hard and strong. The **Rev Janet Fisher** is a graceful person, and she's certainly upright and strong. And remember her part in the Millennium Wood? She got the village to provide saplings and persuaded the Aldridges to spare the land.

very strong and hard-wearing, and its acorns are much enjoyed by pigs.

This sounds like my brother-in-law **Phil Archer**. He's been steadfast at the heart of Ambridge since 1951 and he's still going

are simple with a bluntly-pointed tip, and edges like teeth on a saw. It produces crab apples in autumn.

Simple but lovable? One bloke fits that tag perfectly – **Eddie Grundy.** He's a bit on the wild and untended side, too, even though Clarrie does her best. Aye, Eddie's much loved, but certainly dense.

ENGLISH OAK

Oak is known to all as the national tree of England, once used to provide the sturdy load-bearing beams of a house. The bark becomes rough and fissured as it ages. The heartwood is naturally

strong, even if he has slowed down on the work front.

LOMBARDY POPLAR

The Poplar is a tall, thin, elegant tree with a distinguished outline. It's often planted in lines and provides a barrier against wind, dust and noise. Which puts me in mind of **Brian Aldridge** (some say he's 'debonair', but I've never seen it meself), who's set his face against the women in his family over his daughter Debbie's marriage to that Simon fellow. I said to Christine, there'll be plenty more dust and noise to come before that family row gets sorted out.

YEW

Now this evergreen tree is one of our best-loved conifers. Often found in churchyards, it's become a symbol of mourning. The wood was used for the making of archers' bows. It has many branches, a wide, fluted trunk and what I'd call a tenacious hold on life

Now that has to be our **Shula**. As church warden she's often seen around St Stephen's and her Archer birthright means she knows the value of bows made from yew. She mourned Mark's passing but despite all she's been through, she enjoys life and its challenges to the full.

HOLLY

A compact tree with bright green or purplish twigs, every leaf on the lower branches has sharp points. Its red berries were used for pagan celebrations for years, long before they became Christmas decorations.

Kate Aldridge loves that pagan ritual stuff. Chris says she's happiest when left to roam, hoping to find herself, and that's why she's gone to Morocco. 'Eck of a way to go.

SILVER BIRCH

The Silver Birch seeds itself freely. It's a graceful, slender tree, with yellow male catkins which droop. In contrast the female catkins are smaller and stand tall until they get too big, then topple over. It releases lots of small seeds in August. That line dancing woman **Jolene Rogers** springs to mind but I'd better not dwell on her as I understand she's still none too poplar with some!

ELDER

The elder bush grows wild almost everywhere in Britain. Its twigs are angular – sturdy with a thick pith, but somewhat brittle. The sweet-smelling white blossom can be brewed to make a refreshing tea. The flowers are followed by green berries which turn a purply black and are then harvested to make elderberry wine. The old wood is hard and horny in texture.

HORSE CHESTNUT SILVER BIRCH SYCAMORE

HORSE CHESTNUT

One of my favourites since I was a lad, the wonderful, the majestic Horse Chestnut can be seen in parkland throughout Borsetshire. It's often planted in an avenue of trees to display its white, candelabra-like blossoms. By autumn the tree has produced its fruit – conkers – contained within a spiky husk. (They're inedible, mind.)

Nigel's mother **Julia Pargetter** is my choice for this tree. Handsome enough but with quite a spiky husk if cornered.

SYCAMORE

This attractive tall tree with lots of green foliage and pleasant summer fruits seeds profusely and thrives in the British countryside. The wood is clean and durable, and used to make furniture and kitchen utensils.

I think of me sister-in-law **Jill Archer**. She's had to be strong this year what with all the family troubles. Spends a good deal of time using kitchen utensils cooking for the family – and think of all those cakes for Lower Loxley! Unlike poor Chris who longed for kids, Jill has 'seeded profusely'. Her extended family increases year by year.

Poor old **Joe Grundy** didn't like being uprooted. That really made him run wild. I've seen him wandering aimlessly about, collecting fruit from the hedgerows. Joe certainly enjoys a brew – whether it's tea or country wine – but he'd rather have a drop of cider any day.

Nicholas' StarTurn

Nicholas Parsons

The comedy actor and versatile performer **NICHOLAS PARSONS** has a list of credits to his name, from *The Arthur Haynes Show* and *Sale of The Century* to *The Rocky Horror Show*. To Radio 4 listeners he is perhaps best known as the witty and genial chairman of the game show *Just A Minute*.

Not many people know this, but Nicholas is also a keen follower of *The Archers* and as he says, 'an admirer of the high standard the show maintains in both the writing and the acting.'

So, as *Barwick Green* fades away, we invite him to give us, without hesitation, repetition or deviation,his own amusing and original ideas for *Archers* storylines:

HOME FARM

Kate has returned unexpectedly and has brought with her a Moroccan boyfriend called Habib, who she wants to introduce to her family. Jennifer is, of course, delighted to see her wandering daughter again, though not over-enthusiastic about the handsome new boyfriend. Brian is deeply unsettled, and suspicious that Habib is only courting Kate to persuade her to marry him so he can gain British citizenship. He even wonders whether Kate has been offered money to become a token bride and the relationship could all be a sham. This thought occurs to Brian when he discovers that she has accepted money from Habib to pay her fare home and also to buy a property which she wants to share with Habib back in Ambridge and have her daughter, Phoebe, live with her.

THE BULL

Eddie Grundy has been doing the scratch cards in the *Daily Mail*. To his surprise and delight the two amounts on his card correspond with the amount in the newspaper. He has won £50,000. They can pay off their debts. He rushes to The Bull to tell Clarrie and use the phone to contact the newspaper and make his claim. He tells everyone present which includes Sid, Bert Fry, Jack Woolley, Peggy, and Kate who has dropped in to introduce Habib to an English pub, to have a drink on him. Sid advises caution and not to throw his new-found wealth around. In his exuberant state Eddie ignores this advice, and while on the phone puts the scratch card on the bar counter. There is excitement while drinks are set up and Eddie becomes emotional about the good people of Ambridge. Sid suggests he should wait until he gets the money before he buys a round.

Eddie says he phoned the newspaper and now has to post the card. He then discovers it is no longer on the counter. Joe arrives. Eddie meanwhile goes spare, and starts making accusations. Suspicion falls on the stranger, which makes Kate angry and she drags Habib protesting from the pub. Eddie is shouting for the police to be brought in when Bert Fry wanders from a corner of the pub to thank Eddie for the drink and ask what the card he picked from the bar counter is all about. General relief and laughter from most of them, but aggressive remonstration from Eddie directed at Bert for his innocent but foolish act. Bert's ingenuous reply is: 'I wondered what all the hubbub was about. I thought it concerned something valuable, not a bit of card with numbers on it.'

LOWER LOXLEY

Julia Pargetter has been on holiday to Spain and while there met a woman who has introduced her to the joys of naturism. She regales Nigel and Elizabeth with the pleasures to be found in exposing your whole body to the sun and air. Nigel and Elizabeth treat the information with some humour, as another of Julia's fads which will soon pass. They become concerned, however, when told this new friend of hers, Sylvie Passmore, a French woman married to an Englishman but now divorced, is shortly to visit and hopes to stay the night. A certain tension results from this news so Julia agrees her guest should stay at The Bull. Julia will babysit that afternoon so Elizabeth can go out and, as it is a fine day, she will take the twins into the garden. She says they will be kept in the shade, and as a doting grandmother, will see that the babies come to no harm.

THE BULL

Back at The Bull calm has been restored, and Clarrie and Joe are thrilled by Eddie's windfall. Jack Woolley reminds them that Habib was very upset and perhaps Eddie should go in search of Kate and apologise.

JEFFERSON CRABTREE, SOLICITORS, BORCHESTER

Brian is so unsettled by Kate's Moroccan friend he contacts Usha to discover the situation about illegal immigrants and arranged marriages. While informing him of the legal implications, Usha counsels caution as jumping to the wrong conclusions could create all kinds of problems both personally and legally. Brian is still keen to pursue the matter and discover something about Habib's background.

LOWER LOXLEY

Julia is preparing to take the twins into the garden when her friend Sylvie arrives. They all go outside, and as it is a hot sunny day and a secluded garden, Sylvie suggests they follow their instincts and strip off to let the sun and air 'caress their bodies'. It is while they are in this state that Lynda Snell arrives. She is horrified to be received by Julia barely covered up and led into the garden where Sylvie is now 'starkers'. Sylvie assumes Lynda has the same attitude as Julia and extols the virtues of naturism, and how she is an ambassador for the movement and would, with Julia's help, like to bring it to Ambridge. Lynda rushes off to organise a petition to keep something she considers unwholesome away from the village.

THESE STORYLINES MAY NOW BE FOLLOWED IN WHICHEVER WAY THE WRITERS WISH TO TAKE THEM.

fact file

NAME: USHA GUPTA
BORN: Uganda
ADDRESS: Blossom Hill Cottage
OCCUPATION: Solicitor
FAMILY: Usha's parents and her Auntie Satya live in Wolverhampton. Brother Shiv lives in Leicester
HOBBIES: Salsa dancing, gardening
PAST SINS: More sinned against than sinning

Highs

1991 New to Ambridge, she wins friends by giving a talk to the WI on the Indian Way of Life.
1993 Gives Pip Archer a silk christening gown and cuts the first slice of the special cake.
1994 Buys Blossom Hill Cottage.
1999 Has professional success when Tommy Archer is acquitted of criminal damage charges for trashing his uncle's trial GM crop.

Lows

1994 Is devastated when her solicitor partner Mark Hebden dies in a car crash. She sorts out his affairs with his widow, Shula.
1995 Becomes victim of systematic racist attacks and is sprayed with ammonia by local gang.
1998 Furious to discover Richard Locke is having a wild affair with Shula.

What if...

Richard hadn't noticed Shula?

Souad Faress

Souad thinks it's time Usha pepped up her social life and her love life. 'Usha should be courted by lots of different men,' she says. 'She really needs some attention. She deserves to be spoilt.'

Born in Accra, Ghana, Souad moved as a child to the seaside resort of Southport in Lancashire, where she succumbed to bouts of pneumonia. When a great aunt took her to see *White Horse Inn*, she was overwhelmed by the colour, music and dancing and as soon as she was old enough, headed off to the Guildhall School of Music in London.

TV appearances have included *EastEnders, Prime Suspect II, Inspector Morse, Hijack to Mogadishu* and *Shalom! Salaam*, while for radio she was in *Celestial Cow*, and *Whose Is The Kingdom?* Her film credits include *My Beautiful Laundrette, Journey of No Return* and the title role in *Third Woman*.

Most of Souad's other interests are work-related, including writing and the theatre. She loves snakes and is terrified of spiders. Like her *Archers* character, she is involved in community activities and her charity interests include SANE, the Rural Racism Equality Action Programme (RREA) and asthma charities.

Attractive solicitor Usha Gupta arrived from London in 1991, as Mark Hebden's new partner in his legal practice. Usha found Mark's wife Shula rather daunting, but she persevered and they became friends. At first, she thought the pace of village life rather slow. However, getting to know people in The Bull, and having supper with Jill and Phil, made Usha realise that Ambridge provided the perfect antidote to the long hours she worked in the busy Borchester firm.

Usha was delighted when Ruth and David Archer wanted her to be godmother to their daughter Pip, although, as a Hindu, she had to decline. However, like the good fairy, at the christening she presented Pip with a beautiful gown to wear, gave Pip her blessing, and ceremonially cut the first slice of the splendid cake Jill had made.

Usha decided to live in Ambridge and bought Blossom Hill Cottage, but had to rethink her future when Mark died. She eventually opted to merge the law practice with Felpersham-based solicitors Jefferson Crabtree.

Usha stayed on at the cottage in Ambridge and soon became romantically involved with the dishy doctor, Richard Locke. Her brother Shiv was one of the few who had reservations about Richard and never truly approved of the relationship, although he did his best to like the doctor for his sister's sake.

Not everyone was pleased to see Usha in Ambridge, and she became the victim of systematic racist attacks. Her car was broken into, manure delivered, graffiti scrawled on the cottage wall, and finally she was sprayed with ammonia. Richard's protective instincts were so aroused by this foul treatment, that he realised it was love, and moved in with her.

Eventually, a local gang including Roy Tucker was found to be responsible. Although she came to understand that the naïve Roy had been led astray by thugs, Usha found it hard to forgive him. But she was at least able to offer him help when he needed it, representing him in his paternity battle with Kate Aldridge.

As well as splitting her time between the Borchester and Felpersham offices, Usha is studying for her Higher Court Advocacy Rights qualification, which will enable her to carry out the work of a barrister in a Crown Court.

Sadly, while all Usha's attention was on her work, Richard fell in love with Shula Hebden and the two had a torrid affair. When Shula rejected Richard he left Ambridge for Manchester.

Horrified, Usha found Richard and Shula's treachery hard to bear. It was left to Ruth Archer to get her back in circulation, although a salsa class wasn't the first remedy that sprang to Ruth's mind! Usha's Auntie Satya was in her element, providing delicious food and caustic advice in equal quantities.

Amid a great deal of publicity, Usha's client Tommy Archer was acquitted when he was charged with damaging a test plot of genetically modified oil seed rape belonging to Brian Aldridge.

Forthright, clever and caring, Usha has brought much practical and emotional support to her many Ambridge clients.

GRACE SPEAKS!

SHE'S BACK FROM THE DEAD

Grace Archer's dramatic death was as much of a shock to Ysanne Churchman who played her as it was to the audience, reports **KATE WILLMOTT**

KATE WILLMOTT: Had you any idea of what was going to happen to the newly-married Grace Archer?

YSANNE CHURCHMAN: *I was told that the part of Grace would finish three months before, but not how. Divorce and death seemed out of the question, I thought perhaps she'd lose the power of speech or something! It was very unnerving.*

KW: Did her death come as a shock to you?

YC: *When I read the script at lunchtime on the fateful Thursday I knew the worst. They were killing me off.*

KW. Could you believe it?
YC: *I was under no illusion. It was for real.*

Reunited – Ysanne Churchman and Norman Painting relive the fateful 1955 broadcast 20 years later for the TV cameras

KW: So you were at the centre of the action for the last time.

YC: Afterwards the photographers took pictures of me shaking hands with Harry Oakes (Dan Archer). I don't remember them taking me and Norman Painting (Phil Archer).

KW: The cast didn't take you off for a medicinal drink after the photographs?

YC: No. I think they felt I had become untouchable. If it had happened to me it might happen to them. It shook everyone. The team went their separate ways.

KW: What did you do?

YC: My husband Tony Pilgrim had been at the cinema. He knew the plot was finishing that day. He picked me up from the studio and we travelled back to stay with my parents in Kent.

KW: Did you hear the episode go out that evening?

YC: No, we weren't able to hear the episode go out, but listened to the Omnibus edition. I wanted to hear my

dying words 'I love you Phil'. They had been taken out of the Omnibus. Perhaps the producers thought they were too gruelling to be heard again in view of the response.*

KW: You mean they'd edited it out?

YC: I think so. Twenty years later Norman and I re-enacted the scene for television, and for the radio archives, and I was able to say 'I love you Phil' once more.

KW: How did you cope in the days immediately following Grace's demise?

YC: The Press followed me about for days but were actually very understanding. When I said 'No comment' they left me alone and just took my picture. Nowadays I wouldn't have fared as well, as the treatment from the Press isn't as kind.

KW: Were you ready for listeners' reactions?

YC: I was flabbergasted that the event in Ambridge made such hot news, and of course flattered. It was a really strange time.

KW: Did you get letters?

YC: I received lots of angry letters saying, how dare I give up the part.

KW: Did your career suffer?

YC: One door closes, another door opens. The day Grace died commercial television started. They needed people with voice-over experience, which I'd had from days of voice dubbing for films. So I got lots of television voice-over work.

KW: How do you remember that day?

YC: Norman presented me with a coffin plate sent in to the programme. It reads: In Memory of Grace Archer died 22 September 1955. Age unknown. The age unknown bit is very sweet, I think.

KW: Where do you keep it?

YC: For years I kept it on the mantelpiece at home, but now it's safely locked away.

KW: But that wasn't the end of *The Archers* for you, was it?

YC: No, I didn't lose touch with the programme. Fifteen years later I came back in and played policeman's wife Barbara Drury, then Mary Pound, the deep-voiced woman in a cloth cap, driving her husband's tractor with a cigarette in her mouth, for 14 years – much longer than the three years I spent as Grace.

KW: You see Norman now, don't you?

YC: Tony and I enjoy our annual get-together with Norman on our day, 22 September. Norman keeps me up to date with Archers gossip.

How the media reported Grace's demise:

Listeners sob as Grace Archer dies.
Daily Sketch

Someone travelling by car from Ashford to Dover saw people in villages standing at their doors openly weeping for Grace
Daily Mirror

This was a silly, cheap, unworthy way of getting BBC publicity on the night ITV opened.
News Chronicle

I thought I was in for a lively party when I was invited next door for the first night of ITV. Instead, it was like a house of mourning...
Daily Mirror

BBC Appeal: No more flowers should be sent.

Who are the guilty men?

These are the men who planned the death:
Denis Morris, *Head of Midland Regional Programmes*
Rodney Pelletier, *Head of Light Programme.*
Tony Shryane, the scriptwriters and **Godfrey Baseley.**
Daily Mail

A family in Romney were said to be collecting flowers to make into wreaths and crosses
Daily Mirror

BBC switchboards were jammed. A doctor claimed the shock had damaged the nation's health, the matron of an old folk's home complained that her charges were too upset to sleep and the manager of a West Bromwich factory claimed the 'death' had held up production.

Why do this to Grace Archer?
Daily Express

Imagine the sympathy required of the [BBC] duty officer in charge on the night Grace Archer died. Among the callers that evening was a man, who sounded quite young, who seemed beside himself with grief and who after midnight rang up again, this time quite maudlin with drink, moaning into the telephone that his life had been ruined, and finally bursting into tears.
From *Those Vintage Years of Radio* by John Snagge and Michael Barsley.

What *Archers* listeners recall today

'I wasn't even a twinkle in my mother's eye in 1955 but my mum was a boarder at the Royal Blind School in Edinburgh at the time. The girls always listened to *The Archers* (I don't know what the boys did!) The morning after Grace died they could talk of nothing else. The news went round the school like the latest piece of gossip. 'Hey girls, Grace Archer's dead.' It was as if she'd been one of them.'
Morag Morrimo.

'Tender memories still. She can't be dead. The BBC couldn't do that to us – that's what I thought. I told myself when I listened in to the next episode it would all come right. Phil was wrong – Grace would be resuscitated. When she didn't come back to life the shock and grief took a while to come to terms with.'
Colin Montgomery.

'I had to comfort my gran. She was so upset. "Oh that poor girl," she kept saying.' *Sylvia Bentley.*

'I think it was so poignant because she was trying to rescue her horse – it seemed so very British.'
Ivan Widdicombe.

'We were sitting down to watch Channel 9 [ITV], I think it was called, when the lady from next door came knocking on the back door. "Grace is dead," she shouted. That was the end of our viewing for the night!' *Susan Robson.*

'I was allowed to listen to *The Archers* as long as I did my homework, but I'm afraid all thoughts of Maths and French went out of the window that night.'
Mary Smithson.

'I went into the pub and they were all quiet. "What's happened?" I asked.
' "Haven't you heard?" they all said.'
Arthur Winter.

WHERE WERE YOU ON THE NIGHT OF THE FIRE?

KATE WILLMOTT tells the real story behind a dramatic night in *Archers* history – the death of newlywed Grace Archer in that famous fire of 1955

It came as a bolt from the blue. In 1955, the killing of Grace Archer may have rocked Ambridge but it utterly stunned the nation. Just as the series had established itself as the easy-listening story of country folk, the producers axed one of its stars in the most dramatic fashion. Twenty million listeners – the best audience ever – tuned in to hear 25-year-old Grace's final moments. As soap highlights go, it surpasses the shooting of JR for dramatic impact and makes Tiff's demise in *EastEnders* look half-hearted.

The Archers had been running long enough to be a part of many listeners' lives, and the characters were like members of the family. To lose a young girl, a bride of only a few months, in such tragic circumstances, while rescuing her

horse from a fire, came as a terrible shock, and the listening audience reacted accordingly.

It happened on the night ITV was launched – an astute pre-planned strategy, although the BBC innocently denied it at the time. It did however, steal all the headlines and make those creating *The Archers* understand the power that the programme had. Nothing would ever be the same again.

According to William Smethurst in *The Archers, The Official Companion*

> ### GRACE ARCHER
> (Dulce et decorum est pro BBC mori)
>
> She was well-loved, and millions know
> That Grace has ceased to be.
> Now she is in her grave, but oh
> She's scooped the ITV.
> *Manchester Guardian 1955*

(1985): 'At the June script meeting it was decided to kill a major character – precisely on the night ITV began. Secretary Valerie Hodgetts was told not to duplicate or distribute minutes as usual and a shortlist of victims was drawn up.

'On it were Christine Archer, Carol Grey and newlywed Grace. Somebody commented that Grace

was not terribly popular with listeners because she was too independent and disliked the idea of starting a family. The meeting agreed Grace should endear herself to the nation by changing her mind and rapidly becoming pregnant. The writers agreed to twist the emotional knife further by having her die trying to rescue a horse from a stables' fire.'

As Phil Archer, Norman Painting was in the thick of it. Kate Willmott wondered how it affected him:

KATE WILLMOTT: Why was this shocking story of Grace's death planned?

NORMAN PAINTING: *The Archers* was undoubtedly proving to be one of the BBC's top line programmes but it was becoming too predictable. It was decided to give listeners a jolt by killing off one of the characters.

KW: How was Grace's character chosen to die?

NP: There was a hit list, and I was on that list for a time. It was my good luck and Ysanne's [Churchman, who played Grace] bad luck that she was chosen in the end.

KW: Do you think it was a stunt to

take the limelight from the opening of commercial television?

NP: Everyone always says Grace was killed off to steal the headlines from ITV, but as actors we weren't aware of a conspiracy.

KW: How did the production team tackle the problem?

NP: Producer Tony Shryane was very keen on keeping the programmes topical. He wanted to record each programme on the day it went out but this proved impossible because of the actors' commitments elsewhere. It was decided to mount a week of programmes from Broadcasting House in London, written in the morning to incorporate happenings in the lunchtime news, and ready for the actors to read and work on each day around 2pm.

KW: What happened on the fateful day?

NP: The day was 22 September, the Thursday of this week of topical programmes and as I arrived I was greeted by a tearful Ysanne outside Portland Place saying, 'They've done it. They've killed me off.'

KW: What was your reaction?

NP: There was no time to think or talk about it. Even when I'd read my script I didn't really believe it was going to happen. I can only remember there had been a lot of complaints when something dramatic happened on a Friday because listeners then worried and were upset all over the weekend – that's why they chose a Thursday for the death.

KW: Can you go through how it happened?

NP: We rehearsed and recorded the episode and I remember I did say to the editor, Godfrey Baseley, that Phil would not have been able to say the last line to Dan and Christine, 'She died in my arms on the way to the hospital' in the devastated state he would be in. It was too logical. 'What do you want to say?' asked Godfrey. I said I thought it would be better to turn it round and say: '... in my arms, on the way to the hospital. She's dead.' Godfrey agreed and so it went out. No signature tune was played. The episode ended with a stunned silence.

> A cruel death, it would
> not be denied,
> That cut the bonds of love
> so lately tied.
> I did not think the call
> would come so soon,
> I found it night 'ere
> I thought it noon.
> *A listener*

KW: Was there a press conference?

NP: Yes, as soon as we had finished we were ushered in to see the press who had been called in by George Camacho of the Light Programme. The Press listened to the episode entranced and at the end a raincoated *Picture Post* photographer asked 'What have you done about the switchboard?' The bosses replied 'Nothing. Why, what do you mean?' 'They'll be jammed,' he said.

KW: So this hadn't been foreseen by anyone?

NP: The BBC hadn't realised just how hard it would hit the nation and had no contingency plans at all. The photographer was right. The switchboard was jammed for 48 hours.

KW: How did you feel?

NP: I didn't think it would have such impact. At the time it was just another day's work. As far as I can remember we all went our separate ways. We had different things to do.

KW: What did you do after the recording?

NP: I had a bit of supper and then got to bed, ready for the next day's episode. My diary entry for the day reads simply:
London
Archers 2pm
Supper with Doreen
from Opera da Camera

KW: Were you surprised by the public's response?

NP: The papers were full of Grace's death for the next 12 days. Listeners just couldn't take in what had happened. Even the Press was astonished at the response.

KW: What about listeners' letters?

NP: They started to roll in. From 'I want £2.16s 8d as the missus left the geyser on and I had to get the plumber in,' to tales of women having miscarriages and letters of condolence mostly addressed to Dan Archer, asking him to pass on messages to Phil.

KW: How did Ysanne Churchman feel?

NP: Do you know to this day I have never talked to Ysanne about her feelings.

KW: But you are still in contact with one another?

NP: We meet on that day, 22 September, every year to have lunch together, joined by Ysanne's husband Tony Pilgrim. We didn't start these lunches until the 40th anniversary of Grace's death in 1995. Ysanne rang me and suggested that we have a commemorative lunch. It was so enjoyable we decided to meet each year.

KW: In all its 50 years is this your most vivid *Archers* memory?

NP: When they opened me up for my multiple heart bypass operation a few years ago I told the surgeon he would be sure to find that date, 22 September 1955, engraved on my heart.

JOLENE LOVES SID

BUT THERE'S TROUBLE AT THE SIGN OF THE BULL

JOLENE may have won her man but it could be at great cost with a very uncertain future at The Bull.

After the awful discovery of Sid's secret life with Jolene, Kathy tried her best to make a go of it with him but in the end the trip to Blackpool made her realise the marriage was finally over. She took Jamie to temporary lodgings at Bridge Farm and Sid and Kathy endured a difficult couple of weeks with Kathy 'commuting' in to work.

But when she heard that Jolene was starting to work behind the bar, it was the last straw for unhappy Kathy. She decided to take Sid for all she can and if that meant he loses The Bull then that's tough. She's been hurt and now it's payback time.

Sid's had a difficult year. All that lying and deceit takes it out of a man, even when he's as fit as Sid. For months, he rushed from pillar to post, lying his way out of tight corners all the time, trying to satisfy both wife and mistress.

Sid hated all the lies he's had to tell Kathy but he just couldn't stop himself. Listening to Jolene's seductive tones on the telephone, soaping her in the shower, sharing her bed and slowly dancing with her completely alone and naked – she drew him to her even as he tried to be faithful to Kathy.

What chance did Kathy have? Jolene showed Sid a whole new world of warmth and exotic fun which he entered gladly; but underlying it was her very real need and growing love for him. Heady stuff for a man in his mid-fifties.

Looking back Kathy must have been appalled. All the signs were there and painfully obvious once she knew Sid's secret. His many disappearances 'to the gym', endless late nights, the mysterious phone calls, drawn-out trips to the cash and carry, his mood swings, his keenness to attend a supposed Licensed Victuallers do – on a Friday, on his birthday…

It was a hideous moment for Kathy when a depressed and drunken Eddie blurted out to her whose hospitality Sid was really enjoying that night.

Was it a case of sauce for the goose? Kathy's past affair with DS Barry has made it difficult for her to take the moral high ground. On the other hand, since the birth of Jamie she has made a loyal and loving wife and mother – and she fought her corner in some lively skirmishes with Jolene, not that it's done her any good.

Sid is full of regret for what he did to Kathy – and especially to Jamie. And his problems don't stop there. Fallon's resistance made it difficult for Jolene to move straight into The Bull to be with Sid. And not all of his regulars approved of the way in which Jolene took Kathy's place.

But there is one night of the week when they can put their troubles aside for a couple of hours – line dancing night, when they can lose themselves in that good-time music.

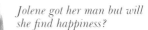

Jolene got her man but will she find happiness?

LINE DANCING WITH SID AND JOLENE

Turn up at The Bull over the last year on the right night and the stomping and yee-hahing that's going on upstairs, led by country 'n' western music singer Jolene Rogers, will leave you in no doubt that Ambridge's favourite keep-fit workout, Line Dancing is a-happening.

As its name suggests Line Dancing is dancing performed in lines using a series of pre-set routine moves. Everyone in the room starts at the same time, dances the same steps as everyone else and finishes at the same time as the music ends – in theory anyway!

Line Dancing keeps you fit, and gives you the confidence and opportunity to meet new friends. The steps are the same for men and women and step sequences once learned will crop up again in other dances.

The accent is on fun – the steps and timing to the music are harder than you think but once you get started there'll be no stopping you. Don't be self-conscious – you can Line Dance as a family, or go on your own as you don't need a partner.

WHAT TO WEAR

A checked shirt, jeans or swirling skirt, and cowboy boots are the order of the day for Ambridge folk bent on having fun along with their exercise.

If you can't run to boots any shoes with leather soles will do as they make the right stomping noise, but don't wear trainers. They make the turns hard to carry out.

BEGINNERS' TIPS

Don't stand at the back of the class, or halfway through the dance you could find yourself at the front, leading the dancers! It's best to stand in the middle as you may turn to face all four walls before the dance is over.

Start with your feet together facing the same way as all the other dancers. Try and remember which move you will make first and make sure you have your weight on the appropriate foot.

Tuck your thumbs in the waist at the front of your jeans or skirt so that your hands don't hang down by your sides.

Keep your steps neat.

HELEN ARCHER AND HAYLEY JORDAN SOON HAD TOMMY ARCHER DOING A HOP, THRUST AND WIGGLE ON THE DANCE FLOOR, AND SO WILL YOU, SO LET'S GO.

JOLENE AND SID DEMONSTRATE THE AMBRIDGE ELECTRIC SLIDE TO GET Y'ALL STRUTTING YOUR STUFF.

AMBRIDGE ELECTRIC SLIDE

Try this dance to the strains of Joe Diffie's *Prop Me Up Beside the Jukebox* (Sony Music) with a slowish tempo till you get the hang of the steps. Then put on *Cotton Eye Joe* by Rednex (Internal Affairs). This faster tempo will really get you moving.

The slide in the Ambridge Electric Slide is the slide used on an electric guitar to give that authentic country music sound.

THE VINE

The first move to learn is the Vine as this is used in many of the dances. Take it nice and easy. You'll soon get the hang of it.

VINE TO THE RIGHT

Start with the feet together and the weight on your left foot.

1. Move to the side with the right foot, heel to the floor.

2. Cross the left foot behind the right foot, ball of foot to the ground.

3. Move to the side with the right foot, putting your weight on it.

4. Stomp the floor with the heel of your left foot. End up standing on your right foot.

VINE TO THE LEFT

1. Move to the side with the left foot, heel to the floor.

2. Cross the right foot behind the left foot, ball of foot to the ground.

3. Move to the side with the left foot, putting your weight on it.

4. Stomp the floor with the heel of your right foot. End up standing on your left foot.

WALKING BACK

Start with the feet together and the weight on your left foot.

1. Walk backwards on to the right foot.

2. Walk backwards on to the left foot.

3. Walk backwards on to the right foot.

4. Cross the left foot over the right foot and tap.

STEP AND TAP

1. Walk forward on to the left foot.

2. Tap the right foot across and behind the left foot.

3. Walk backwards on to the right foot.

4. Cross the left foot back across the right foot and tap.

THE SCUFF

1. Walk forward on to the left foot, bending the knee slightly.

2. Swing the right leg forward and let the right heel scuff the floor, swivelling the left foot to make a 90 degree turn to the left.

Start the Ambridge Electric Slide again facing the wall that was on your left before.

Dear Julia

Lower Loxley grande dame Julia Pargetter takes time out from her hectic lifestyle to advise on personal dilemmas in business, health or relationships. A former thespian, who has struggled with her own demons – alcohol, gambling, acute snobbery – her solutions are stunningly simple and offered in the unaffected manner characteristic of this one-time wartime variety dancer, sorry, acclaimed West End actress.

I'M NOT A VILLAIN – AM I?

I was indirectly responsible for a family being evicted from their home. I'm not one to kick a man when he's down and I did try to explain the situation to them – they should have read the letters, for God's sake. Now, whenever I see the family or pass their old home I am filled with a terrible feeling of guilt. I am finding it very hard to come to terms with this. What can I do? B.A.

Be a man not a mouse. If you did all you could at the time with warnings and an explanation you have nothing to reproach yourself for. Time is a great healer and you'll probably find that this family will realise you were not the wicked villain after all. In the meantime, a sober assessment of your personal code of ethics and what's left of your integrity probably won't do any harm. My leaflet, Do I Have A Conscience? should help.

HOW CAN I MOTIVATE THEM?

I am in charge of organising our village fete which is usually quite a big affair. Although I am an experienced organiser, particularly in the field of amateur dramatics, my problem is getting other people motivated. I can't be expected to do it all on my own and yet others seem reluctant to help whenever one suggests that perhaps they might pitch in. L.S.

I know exactly how you feel. I too am excellent at organising and no one gives me the appreciation I deserve either. The fault is theirs, not yours. Take a firm line. Ring them up, e-mail them, call round personally, but whatever you do, don't let them off the hook. They'll thank you for it in the end. If all else fails offer free bottles of champagne. You'll be surprised at the response. And put my name at the head of the list.

SHOULD TRUE LOVE WAIT?

I am young, fun-loving and very fond of my boyfriend with whom I have a very good relationship. Now we are planning to move in together and I am really looking forward to it but there is a chance that the mother of his lovely two-year-old daughter might return – she has been travelling abroad for several months – and then where would I be? H.J.

Just remember that possession is nine points of the law. If this boy wants you to move in with him, then he obviously feels strongly for you – now. Keep it that way. NEVER let him see you without make-up or wearing those awful leggings young women today are so fond of – and then before you know where you are you'll be married and living happily ever after. Then if the baby's wayward mother returns it will be too late. She'll be the one with the problems.

MUMMY TROUBLE

My wife and I have had some measure of success in our family business and have succeeded in expanding it into new areas. The trouble is my mother will insist on interfering. She throws a spanner in the works just when we get things going, and worse, she will keep chatting up the workmen, taking them cups of tea and stopping them getting on with the job. And what's more, she doesn't have a clue about money and carries on spending ours as if we were a family of superannuated aristocrats, not a modest business. What am I to do about mummy? Name withheld.

Handled wisely and with tact a mother can be your best friend. However, your mother sounds, to be blunt, like an interfering old harridan who should be put in her place. The fact that you call her 'mummy' suggests your relationship with her is too close. How does your wife feel about this? However, don't be too harsh where spending is concerned: every woman needs to splash out occasionally, even if it is at Underwoods rather than Harvey Nichols. Pull back, ignore what she says, and you may find she'll shut up and go away for a spell.

(This is such a common complaint that I shall be giving it my full attention in our next issue.)

PAIN IN THE BACK

Although I am well past the first flush of youth I am still quite an active woman and enjoy the outdoor life. For more than a year, I've been troubled with my back which has gradually grown worse, so much so that I've had to stop riding, which is my job as well as my favourite recreation. I have been to my GP who gave me painkillers and sent me to a physiotherapist but my back gets no better. I am at my wits' end. C. B.

You should go back to your GP and tell him the situation. He might suggest seeing an osteopath, in which case I can recommend a local one who has put me straight more than once. Send me a stamped addressed envelope for details.

INHARMONIOUS LIFESTYLE

My wife and I have stood together through thick and thin, including losing my business and her having to go out to work. But now I can take no more. She has become completely obsessed with the Chinese teaching feng shui. Everything in the house has been moved around, different coloured objects have been hung from the walls and even the bed has been moved to a new 'more harmonious' position. I liked it as it was. I never want to hear the words feng shui again. And as for The Mikado...don't get me started. R.S.

I know it must be hard for you, but women do get bees in their bonnets about curious things, as do men. Have you never seen a living room full of football supporters' scarves and trophies? Or an extension devoted to the glory days of the Triumph Stag? Don't waste your happy years together – go back to her and indulge her in her fantasies. It could be worse. She might be notching up other men on her suspender belt! And for that matter when did you last see her suspender belt?

Julia Pargetter

Julia Pargetter is not able to enter into individual correspondence and can only answer letters via this page. She can only deal with written requests.

LIFESKILLS
with **Helen Archer**

The other day I was e-mailed a healthy reminder as to why women in business have to beware. Read on!

WHY WOMEN RULE THE WORLD

We got off the *Titanic* first.

We can scare male bosses with mysterious gynaecological disorder excuses.

We can cry and get off speeding fines.

Taxis stop for us.

Free drinks, free dinners, free movies (you get the point).

New lipstick gives us a whole new lease of life.

If we're not too bright, some people will find it cute.

We've never been duped by a Wonderbra.

The trouble with this kind of stuff is that it's funny. It's the thinking behind it which is so dangerous. If you want to shoot to the top in the business world today you have to deal with the structure as it is.

Think like a man, talk like a man, fight your case like a man, and make sure that everyone has heard about you, especially the boss. When that strategy works – and believe me, it will – then you can get down to changing one or two things. But it won't be the colour of your nail varnish and you can never ever rely on your Wonderbra to underpin a presentation.

Don't get me wrong, I'm all for using womanly wiles if nothing else will get you your way, but you have to know exactly what you're doing and only act cute, cry or flash your cleavage when it's to your advantage. And remember – if your boss is female she'll either be scared of the competition or see right through you.

Pin this advice on the notice board and be warned: The way to get ahead is not to play dumb.

From the Postbag
Babes and Sucklings

I'm in organic pork and am involved in making and selling sausages. My older sister is a bossy boots and keeps telling me what to do. Should I let her or do you reckon she'll cramp my style?
Tom Archer, Bridge Farm

Keep doing as she tells you and you'll be fine. What style?

That Don't Impress Me Much

Thank you for your reply to my last letter. I've made the list like you said. But I don't reckon I'm gonna get no qualifications. Where does that leave me?
Edward Grundy, Ambridge

Out in the cold. Sorry.

Pig in a Poke?

What do you do with a wife who tells you to get a white-collar job when all you want to do is work on the land, preferably with pigs?
Neil Carter, The Green

Change your wife or your job – whichever you think's most important. But draw up a game plan first.

ROUTE TO THE

NIFTY EDITS
Expert work edits all the morning's errors very swiftly.
Move forward 2 spaces.

7

SELF DOUBT
Was that birdsong in the Lakey Hill scene correct for this time of year? Check surreptitiously.
Yes it was!
Extra go.

8

BOOST THE EGO
Encouraging words from Editor and members of the cast give new actor more confidence. Scenes go well.
Move forward 5 spaces.

GRUNDY TROUBLE
Offer cast and team post-production drinks in the BBC bar. Out of cash and credit cards are in other coat. Murmurs of 'Not again!' all round.
Go back three spaces.

10

REPEAT PERFORMANCE
Radio 4 on in office during lunch break. Help. They're putting out the wrong episode. I've heard this before. 'Course I have. It's the repeat. Silly me!
Miss a turn.

6

You are a Producer of *The Archers*.

BAD LUCK
Editing computer SADIE goes down.
Is there a back-up?
Yes, there is.
Miss a turn then move forward 2 spaces next turn.

11

FIRST NIGHT NERVES
New actor very nervous, causing several re-takes during recording.
Run over time.
Go back one space.

5

You have to go through all the pitfalls and problems of getting an episode recorded in time and on air.

WOT A SHAME
Cast assemble for read-through. Episode far too long.
Major cuts required.
Go back 1 space.

4

WHERE HAVE THEY GONE?
Two scripts returned 'unknown'. Actors have moved without telling us. Frantic phone calls to find new addresses. Where do we send their cheques?
Go back 2 spaces.

CONGRATULATIONS
Everyone says the 50th Birthday special script is a cracker.
Send scripts out to actors and production crew.
Move on 3 spaces.

Can YOU do it?!?

FLYING START
Off to a good start – completed scripts arrive from writers on time.
Move on 3 spaces.

AIRWAVES

21 MANY CONGRATULATIONS

50th Birthday special script transmitted to four and a half million listeners. Critics full of praise.

SATISFACTORY TRANSMISSION.
Put your feet up and take a look at the next set of scripts.

WEATHER FLASH
Severe weather flash MUST be broadcast after 7pm news. Programme delayed 30 seconds. Miss a turn.

20

19 PHEW! DISASTER AVERTED
Agricultural news postponed. Deep sigh of relief. Move on 2 spaces.

Rules

a. Using tiddlywinks or buttons, choose a counter and place on **START.**

b. Highest throw on the dice goes first.

c. Follow the instructions at the space you land on. Next player throws the dice.

d. The first Producer to get to the Satisfactory Transmission circle wins!

12 HURRAY!

Check timings. Each episode running between 12.20 and 12.40 to end of speech plus 57 seconds of closing music. Perfect.
Move on 4 spaces.

DISASTER STRIKES
Warned of possible farming news which will make nonsense of today's episode.
Go back 2 spaces.

18

SAVED
Programme DAT found – filed in wrong slot. Cancel back-up facilities, but Editor on the warpath. Get out of the way quickly! Move on 1 space.

17

WELL DONE
Transmission copy and programme details sent to London well in time. Move on 1 space.

13

PANIC STATIONS!
Programme missing from today's slot in tape library. Set up stand-by arrangements to use back-up copy sent 'down the line' from Birmingham to London.
Move back 2 spaces.

16

ANGEL
Cleared up all post-production paperwork earlier than usual. Put on halo.
Move forward 3 spaces.

15

KNOT IN HANKY
Forgotten about the Bank Holiday. Scheduling up the spout.
Go back 3 spaces.

fact file

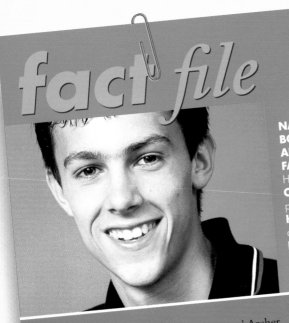

NAME: THOMAS (TOMMY) ARCHER
BORN: 25 February 1981
ADDRESS: Bridge Farm, Ambridge
FAMILY: Son of Pat and Tony, brother to Helen, and John (deceased)
OCCUPATION: Organic pig farmer/part-time student
HOBBIES: DJ at discos, ecology, having a good time
PAST SINS: Held in prison for wrecking a GM trial crop on his Uncle Brian's land. Met girlfriend against court's instructions

Tommy Archer

Highs

1997 Organises GCSE results rave in Village Hall which goes wrong but brother John gets the flak for making the booking.
1998 Ambridge Originals organic pork and leek sausages go into production after they prove popular at Royal Show.
1999 Falls for Kirsty Miller, fellow destroyer of GM trial crops, but enforced absence made the heart grow colder.

Lows

1998 Brother John dies in a tractor accident on Tommy's birthday.
1999 Falls out with Hayley, his partner in the organic pig enterprise, thanks to sister Helen's interference.
1999 Charged with causing £42,000 damage to GM trial crop but acquitted.

What if...

Tommy's principles get him into trouble again?

Tom Graham

Tom got the part of Tommy Archer in the autumn of 1997. As a member of Central Television's Junior Workshop, he was studying for his A-levels, having attained nine As and Bs in his GCSEs – considerably better than young Tommy Archer.

Tom is now at Manchester University where he combines his studies with acting. In the vacations he plays guitar/vocals in a three-piece band called Homebaked, performing in Midland clubs and at festivals.

It won't be 'young Tommy' Archer for much longer. Twenty in February, the second son of Pat and Tony Archer of Bridge Farm now prefers to be called 'Tom' and is quickly taking his place in Ambridge as part of the up-and-coming generation.

He's well into his studies at Borsetshire Agricultural College where he attends one day a week. The rest of the time he's working on his parents' farm or occasionally helping out at the organic shop in Borchester. Sadly for him, his birthday will always be associated with the death of his older brother John who was killed in a tractor accident on that day in 1998.

Although Tommy is a likeable and well-meaning lad he has already had his share of trouble. He was involved in a rowdy drinking spree in Ambridge Village Hall where more than 300 teenagers had gathered to celebrate their GCSE results. About £200 damage was done and it came to light that Tommy had persuaded his elder brother John to book the hall without telling him about the rave. The police were involved and warnings given, but no one was arrested. Tommy remained quietly nursing a hangover.

Two years later Tommy surprised everyone when he was charged with causing criminal damage to a trial crop of genetically modified oil seed rape on the farm of his uncle, Brian Aldridge. No one, least of all his parents, had been aware of just how passionately he felt about the issue. He was convinced that the crop would affect fields in neighbouring farms, including the organic Bridge Farm and got together with like-minded friends to trash it.

He then spent an extremely uncomfortable few months worrying about whether he would go to prison. He was found not guilty of causing criminal damage, although some of Ambridge's more conservative residents thought he deserved at least a public ticking off, but he won't forget his experience on remand in a hurry.

Hayley Jordan, who used to be John's girlfriend, stood by Tommy and they grew even closer when together they organised the manufacture and sale of sausages produced from their own organically-reared pork. Initially John's project, they wanted to continue it in his memory.

Then just when it looked as though the scheme might take off, Pat and Tony, prompted by manipulative daughter Helen, decided that it must be part of the overall Bridge Farm output, and Hayley could not be a partner. The organic sausages are now marketed as Bridge Farm Originals and Helen keeps a firm grip on her brother's entrepreneurial activities.

Tommy is working hard on the farm and hoping the family's organic shop in Borchester will increase his pork and sausage sales. Like John, he has no trouble attracting the opposite sex but isn't talkative about his girlfriends. His relationship with Kirsty, another protester against trials of GM crops, foundered when they were forced to stay apart under her bail conditions.

By the time Kirsty's case was dropped, there was a problem – the shapely but not very bright Lauren...

Golden Oldies

*Ambridge's original country folk, from the redoubtable
Mrs P to the wily Ned Larkin, are still fondly remembered
half a century on*

Mrs Perkins,
known to all as
Mrs P (Pauline Seville)

Few women can have married two different men with the same surname, yet that is exactly what Polly Perkins, mother of Peggy Archer, did. When Polly's first husband Albert died in 1951, Peggy insisted that her mother leave London and join her in Ambridge.

After her life in London's East End, you'd have expected her to feel like a fish out of water in leafy Ambridge. But no, the redoubtable Mrs Perkins soon settled into village life and busied herself minding everyone else's business. She wore black, carried an umbrella, and was renowned for always speaking her mind, no matter what was on it or how unpleasant the consequences for other people.

She was swiftly accepted as 'Mrs P', and became as much a part of Ambridge as those who had lived there for a lifetime. She had no time for son-in-law Jack's drinking habits, but gave plenty of backing to her granddaughter Jennifer. Although she was shattered when Jennifer had an illegitimate child, Mrs P never wavered in her support, despite the challenge to her own moral code.

There were plenty of suitors for this middle-aged Cockney sparrow, undeterred by her forked tongue and forthright manner. She had a long and colourful arm's-length relationship with Walter Gabriel. She always referred to him as 'Mr Gabriel', and he in turn spoke respectfully to her as 'Mrs P ma'am.'

It was Arthur Perkins, the stone mason and teetotaller, who finally succeeded in getting her hand in marriage and making her Mrs Perkins for the second time. They moved to London for a few years but Arthur was not in good health and died after a heart attack. Once again Mrs P found her way back to Ambridge but times had changed and she was lonely. She died peacefully at home in 1991.

She may have been Mrs Perkins twice, but there will only ever be one 'Mrs P.'

INSIDE STORY
*Pauline Seville was at least 20 years younger than
the character she played, and as gentle and kindly as
Mrs P was fierce. After her death, Pauline received one
of the programme's chief accolades – no one was re-cast
to play her part.*

Ned Larkin
(Bill Payne)

Ned Larkin bounced on to the Ambridge scene in 1956 when Dan Archer was looking for a replacement for his trusty farmhand Simon Cooper, who was retiring.

Help was at hand in the shape of Ned, who already lived in Ambridge with his wife Mabel and their five children. He was soon a fixture at Brookfield, and became one of the series' best-loved comic characters. The formidable Mabel did her best to keep order when she wasn't cleaning for Doris Archer or helping Carol Grey with her market garden.

Ned's younger brother Bob was always in trouble, and usually managed to involve Ned too. He came to stay with Ned and Mabel, mostly because Ned thought he should meet Pru Harris, 'a nice quiet type of girl' who might keep him on the straight and narrow.

Pru was more interested in Tom Forrest, but the matter was brought to a tragic end when Bob was discovered poaching by Tom and Phil Archer. In the struggle that followed Bob was shot and killed. Tom was charged with his manslaughter and acquitted, but it was a long time before Ned could talk to Tom or accept that his brother had been 'a wrong 'un'.

Ned did remain firm friends with Walter Gabriel, and the two of them were involved in a number of escapades. The most memorable of these was the 'ghost' of Arkwright Hall, which terrified the two men and turned out to be a gypsy who'd been squatting there. On another occasion Ned fell through the floor of the hall and discovered a number of gold sovereigns – not enough to make him rich, however.

On Ned's retirement, he and Mabel moved into Woodbine Cottage, but sadly he died shortly after in 1967. In the way things go in Ambridge, their son Jethro was to take his father's place at Brookfield, and Jethro's daughter, Clarrie, became Mrs Eddie Grundy.

INSIDE STORY

Bill Payne lived in Warwickshire and was as much of a legend locally as the character he played nationally. He's still talked of affectionately in the fish and chip shop in Stratford-upon-Avon and remembered for his fund of stories and jokes, told with a completely straight face. Just when everyone believed him he would crack up, roaring with laughter. He was a great one for making his fellow actors laugh in the middle of a 'take' which endeared him to them if not to the production team!

Laura Archer
(Gwenda Wilson)

It must have come as a terrible shock to the Archer family when a distant relative from New Zealand announced that she was about to descend on them to start a new life. Laura Archer was the widow of Dan's brother, Frank, who had emigrated to New Zealand's South Island where he had been a successful sheep farmer.

After Frank died, Laura decided to return to her husband's family roots where she expected to be greeted with open arms. As it was, 'Aunt Laura,' as she became known, was greeted with a certain amount of hostility, mostly brought on by her belligerent manner and 'know it all' attitude to farming.

She channelled these talents into running every organisation in the county, and handing out portions of her considerable personal fortune. She enabled Jack and Peggy to buy the freehold of The Bull, which pleased them, and then had an extension built so that she could move in, which pleased them rather less.

Laura bought what became Ambridge Hall and was delighted when Colonel Danby – Freddie, as she called him – moved in as a paying guest. The two managed to form a relationship, of a sort, with the possibility of marriage being touched upon but never taken very seriously. She wanted Freddie to inherit the hall when she died in 1985, but, typically, failed to make this clear in her will and it went instead to a relation in New Zealand.

It was more than appropriate that after Aunt Laura's barn-storming years in Ambridge, Ambridge Hall should be bought by another forthright lady with a will of her own, Lynda Snell. For Aunt Laura, the lamp still burns.

INSIDE STORY

'When Gwenda Wilson died I could not believe that her energy and enthusiasm would no longer be there to enliven the recordings. I had to decide what to do about the recordings already made with her. Finally, you make the decision and the recordings go out. Her voice comes up…as Aunt Laura, the crotchety old busybody of Ambridge. What have you done? That's not how you want her to be remembered… Gwenda was an actress and that was another of her wonderful performances. And that is how she would want to be remembered.'
Tony Shryane, producer of The Archers for 28 years, in the BBC magazine Ariel, shortly after the death of Gwenda Wilson.

Martha Woodford
(Mollie Harris)

Just before her arrival in Ambridge, Martha's life had been marred by tragedy. The loss of her husband of 30 years, Penny Hassett postman Herbert Lily, was followed soon after by the death of their baby son.

In the village, she took on all manner of work to make a living. First she worked at the Field Study Centre at Arkwright Hall but she came up against gardener Zebedee Tring, who detested women in general, and Martha was given the sack. It was while she was working as a petrol pump attendant at Ralph Bellamy's garage that she agreed to marry Joby Woodford. They were married on Christmas Day 1972.

Jack Woolley asked Martha to run the Ambridge Post Office and Village Shop, a job she enjoyed and made very much her own. By its very nature the Village Shop is the centre of all that goes on, and Martha Woodford certainly knew all the gossip.

Widowed for the second time, the still-attractive Martha was not short of male company, but she gave up working in the shop when Jack Woolley's constant interference and the vagaries of VAT proved too much for her.

After a short stay with Marjorie Antrobus, when the two women just did not get on, she moved into April Cottage.

Martha continued to play a lively part in village life, knitting scarves and gloves for whoever needed them, being an active member of the Over-Sixties, and occasionally filling in at the shop for Betty Tucker. She is still remembered for the loving care she gave Ambridge's red telephone box, polishing it until it shone and leaving flowers daily.

When Martha died in 1995, it was as though a little of the village died with her.

INSIDE STORY

Much of writer, countrywoman, and broadcaster Mollie Harris shone through into the character of Martha Woodford. Mollie said of her: 'Martha is a kind person. She's not a malicious gossip. She just passes it on.'

Mollie loved flowers and she always wore a flower from her abundant garden in her buttonhole when she attended recordings. She was a genuine countrywoman and crowded among the more formal bouquets at her funeral was a mass of flowers picked from hedgerows – a silent tribute to an unusual personality.

Carol and John Tregorran
(Anne Cullen and Basil Jones)

John and Carol arrived in the same year, and broke the mould of traditional characters, for they were neither conventional 'country-folk' nor stereotyped 'townies'.

John's debut was surprising. His gypsy caravan had broken a wheel and he was left on the outskirts of Ambridge not even sure where he was. The villagers were suspicious, particularly when horses went missing.

He turned out to be a university lecturer, whose win on the football pools had enabled him to resign and wander the countryside at his leisure. Before long Ambridge was very fond of him. He took an active part in village activities and became a parish councillor.

Carol Grey took the village by storm when she arrived from Surrey, having bought a smallholding from Dan Archer that his son Jack had let go. 'Miss Grey' allowed nothing to stand in her way, especially the 'Get it done tomorrow' attitude of the locals.

The smallholding became a market garden and Jack Archer returned to work for 'Miss Grey'. The one thing that puzzled people was that there was no man in her life.

This changed when one day she rounded a corner in her little car and knocked John Tregorran off his motor scooter. He'd already had several girlfriends in Ambridge, including Christine Archer, but in Carol he found someone his intellectual equal, as well as attractive.

Their friendship blossomed, but not sufficiently for Carol to accept John's proposal of marriage. She married Charles Grenville and had a son, Richard, by him, and soon after John married district nurse Janet Sheldon.

The four remained firm friends until Janet was killed in a car crash. Charles died on a business trip to America, leaving the house and a legacy to Carol.

Twelve years after the first proposal, Carol became Mrs John Tregorran and three years later their daughter Anna Louise was born. But marriage didn't bring complete happiness. On one occasion Carol was accused of shoplifting but acquitted, and later John appeared to be getting rather too involved with Jennifer Aldridge.

Eventually, John and Carol went to live in Bristol, leaving Ambridge with more than 30 years of memories.

INSIDE STORY

The eternally popular John Tregorran was played by five actors over the years – Basil Jones, Philip Morant, Simon Lack, John Bott and Roger Hume. Anne Cullen as Carol took her husband's multiple personalities in her stride – perhaps because in real life she was married to Monty Crick, one of four actors to play Dan Archer!

Colonel Danby
(Norman Shelley / Ballard Berkeley, above)

It was by chance that Lieutenant-Colonel 'Freddie' Danby made his home in Ambridge. Retired, he was area representative for a national charity and answered Laura Archer's advertisement for a paying guest at Ambridge Hall.

He agreed to stay for a month and remained in Ambridge for many years.

He and Aunt Laura settled into a mutually convenient domesticity, and although he gentlemanly offered her his hand in marriage, he was relieved when she refused.

When his charity work ended Freddie took on a succession of lowly jobs in order to make ends meet. When Laura became ill he took on the domestic chores, including cooking.

Through an oversight in the will, Freddie did not inherit Ambridge Hall when Laura died. Instead it went to a distant relative in New Zealand who was only too happy for Freddie to remain as a tenant.

But this was more than Freddie could afford, so he moved into a bungalow in Manorfield Close. What he hadn't bargained for was the unwanted attention of the widows of Ambridge who, despite his years, saw this upright unattached Army officer as a good catch.

He fled in 1986 to stay with an old Army colleague in Bristol but will be long remembered in Ambridge, especially for his performances in the pantomimes staged by the Ambridge Players.

INSIDE STORY

Norman Shelley and Ballard Berkeley played this most charming of characters. Ballard portrayed the eccentric Major in Fawlty Towers *and Norman Shelley voiced the speeches of Winston Churchill for wartime broadcast to America. Norman had a daily ritual during recording. He carried a small briefcase containing a whisky decanter and a cut glass beaker. When the mood took him he would unlock the briefcase, wipe the glass with a clean cloth, and take a small snifter of whisky. Having neatly tossed back the whisky out would come the cloth, back in the case would go the glass and a twinkling Norman would embark on another anecdote.*

Fifty years of presenting
The Archers

Fascinating Facts

◆ First there was a week of pilot programmes starting on Whit Monday, 29 May 1950 and heard only on the Midland Home Service. *The Archers of Wimberton Farm* went out at 4–4.15pm.

◆ Godfrey Baseley made a special long trail for the BBC Light Programme, which went out at 5.30pm on 28 December 1950, and was called *Introducing The Archers*, to prepare listeners for the first national broadcast (see page 66).

◆ *The Archers* started on 1 January 1951 at 11.45am on the Light Programme. It was given three months until Friday 23 March 1951 to prove its worth.

◆ The signature tune *Barwick Green* was on a Boosey & Hawkes 'mood music' green label disc. Its first four bars were cut and have never been used in the programme.

◆ For the first episode, the announcer's famous introduction 'The Archers. An everyday story of country folk' was followed by an introduction to Dan, Doris and family.

◆ The series moved to the prime spot of 6.45pm at Easter 1951 with two million listeners. It wasn't transmitted on Easter Monday, 26 March, so the very first evening edition went out on Tuesday 27 March. A week later the audience had doubled to four million. By December 1951 it was six million.

◆ The first *Radio Times* picture of *The Archers* was in the Midland edition only, for the week 4–10 November 1951. It showed a fireside scene with Dan, Doris and Christine Archer.

◆ Each episode included an introduction recorded by Birmingham staff announcers Christopher Stagg or Richard Maddock.

◆ The first Omnibus was heard on Saturday 5 January 1952 at 7.30–8.30pm, introduced by Bob Arnold in his role as Tom Forrest. He started with a topical homily about the countryside before saying: 'Now let me tell you what's been going on in Ambridge in the past week.'

◆ In December 1952 there was no transmission of *The Archers* on Christmas Day, consequently there was a 45-minute Omnibus on Saturday 27 December at 7.30pm.

◆ *The Archers* was first heard on the BBC General Overseas Service in summer 1953. A series of special editions was recorded to bring the overseas audience up to date.

- The Omnibus moved to a new time, 8–9pm on Saturdays from 15 October 1955.

- The biggest audience ever – 20 million – was in 1955 for the episode of Grace Archer's death (see page 33).

- The Omnibus was shortened and moved from Saturday evenings to Sunday afternoons for the summer, and was heard at the new time, 3.15–4pm from Sunday 22 July 1956.

- By September 1956 the Omnibus was back to the Saturday evening one-hour slot.

- The first stereo recording experiment was on Saturday 31 October 1964.

- The first lunchtime repeat was heard on the BBC Home Service at 12.40pm in 1965.

- The Home Service evolved into Radio 4 in 1967, so the first Radio 4 Omnibus was heard on 1 October 1967 at 9.30–10.30am (written by Bruno Milna, otherwise known as Norman Painting, and Edward J Mason). On Monday 2 October listeners heard *The Archers* at 1.45pm and 6.45pm.

- The time change from 6.45pm to 7.05pm was instituted by then Radio 4 Controller Ian McIntyre on Monday 26 September 1977.

- The Omnibus moved to a new time of 6.15pm on Sunday 2 October 1977.

- The programme was regularly broadcast in stereo from 8 June 1992. A new version of the signature tune *Barwick Green* was recorded in stereo.

- On Monday 6 April 1998 the evening programme timing changed slightly to 7.02–7.15pm and the lunchtime repeat moved to 2.02pm.

- A sixth episode on Sunday night was introduced on Easter Sunday, 12 April 1998 at 7.02pm. It ended with a gripping cliff-hanger concerning Daniel's mysterious illness. Shula and Alistair conducted a vigil at Daniel's bedside. The tests were inconclusive, but it was not meningitis. Dr Locke's visit didn't help as he was not willing to express an opinion. Shula was worried that the doctor knew and wasn't saying. Could it be leukaemia?

- The following week on 19 April 1998 the Omnibus was increased to 75 minutes, from 10–11.15am.

- Members of the armed forces and their families serving overseas hear *The Archers* broadcast locally by the British Forces Broadcasting Service. When Hong Kong was handed back to China, British troops moved out and the local expatriates cried: 'How are we going to hear *The Archers* now…?'

- … on the Internet is the answer. From Sunday 19 November 1999 *The Archers* could be heard on-line anywhere in the world.

- Currently the programme has a brief introduction voiced live in London, followed by the crisp phrase: 'It's *The Archers*.'

(With thanks to Peter Tewkesbury)

THE BRIDGE FARM
— COLLECTION —

THE MARKET FOR ORGANIC PRODUCE IS BOOMING
WHICH IS GOOD NEWS FOR THE BRIDGE FARM ARCHERS.
HERE THEY'VE DEVISED SOME TEMPTING RECIPES USING
THEIR HOME-GROWN PRODUCTS. TRY THEM
– YOU MIGHT BE CONVERTED!

PAT'S FREE RANGE FARMHOUSE CHICKEN

Serves 6

Pat has found a source of hand-reared, free range organic chicken. This gives her an opportunity to use several Bridge Farm products, together with cheese carefully selected from Anne Baxter's Cheese Centre in presenting a dish that her friends agree is one of her best.

Roast the chicken in butter at 200ºC/gas mark 6 for 20 minutes, then turn the bird, rub in more butter, return to the oven, and after an hour the chicken will be ready.

Put all the sauce ingredients on a low heat for ten minutes, constantly stirring. Do not boil.

Carve the chicken into joints. Put a layer of sauce in the dish, then the chicken pieces, then another layer of sauce. Add a few breadcrumbs and a little butter from the chicken and bake in the hottest oven for five minutes. Finish off under a hot grill.

To serve:
This tastes good with dollops of organic mashed potato sprinkled with freshly chopped parsley, and a rocket, avocado and pine kernel salad.

Ingredients
A 1.4kg/3lb chicken

For the sauce:
50g/2 oz Bridge Farm butter
2 tablespoons organic flour
150 ml/¼ pint giblet stock
Fresh rosemary and thyme
2 organic onions, finely chopped
2 organic carrots, finely sliced
6 tablespoons white wine
300ml/½ pint thick Bridge Farm cream
1 dessertspoon grain mustard
4 tablespoons of grated cheese
3 tablespoons breadcrumbs
Salt and pepper

TOMMY'S BRIDGE FARM ORIGINALS HOTPOT

Serves 4

Ingredients

10 Pork and leek
Originals sausages
2 organic onions, sliced in rings
2 organic leeks, washed and sliced
2 organic potatoes
2 tablespoons flour
1 small organic lemon
2 teaspoons paprika
50g/2 oz Bridge Farm butter
300ml/½ pint of stock or water

Tommy Archer is justifiably proud of his Bridge Farm Originals Sausages. They were his idea and are made to his specification. He thought this easy recipe would be ideal for his mates if they wanted to show off their skill at cooking.

Fry the onions and leeks in butter until they are soft but not brown. Remove from the pan and put into a warmed casserole. Parboil the potatoes, then slice and add to casserole.

Cut the sausages into chunks. Put the flour in a polythene bag and shake the chunks in it until well coated. Fry the sausages until they are just beginning to turn brown then transfer into casserole.

Add paprika to the frying pan and stir. Add the lemon juice, salt and stock or water. Bring to the boil and pour over the sausages. Bake in a medium oven 180ºC/gas mark 4 for one and a half hours.

To serve:

Tommy prefers his hotpot to be accompanied by organic carrots, boiled, with a knob or two of butter and some crusty home-made bread.

TONY'S FAVOURITE BLACKBERRY AND YOGHURT CHEESECAKE

Serves 6

Ingredients

40g/1½oz Bridge Farm butter
100g/4 oz organic wheat digestive biscuits, pounded into crumbs
100g/4oz medium fat soft cheese
150g/5oz Bridge Farm natural yoghurt
150ml/¼ pint whipped Bridge Farm double cream
1 (11.7g) sachet gelatine
25g/1oz icing sugar
0.5kg/1lb fresh blackberries, picked by Helen, if you're lucky

As a boy, Tony Archer loved blackberrying with his grandfather Dan Archer on the slopes of Lakey Hill. Now any excuse will do for Tony to indulge himself in this organic fruit. And the combination of digestive biscuits and double cream makes it his favourite dessert.

Melt the butter in a saucepan and mix thoroughly with the biscuit crumbs. Press into a (18cm/7 inch) loose bottomed cake tin and refrigerate until firm.

Save 12 large blackberries for decoration. Cook the rest in a pan with 2 tablespoons of water, until pulped. Allow to cool.

Sprinkle gelatine into 3 tablespoons hot water and whisk briskly until the gelatine dissolves. Allow to cool for a few minutes, stirring occasionally.

Beat yoghurt, sugar and soft cheese together, then fold in the blackberry puree, gelatine and whipped cream. Pour on to the biscuit crust and return the cake tin to the fridge to chill.

To serve:

Remove from cake tin when set. Decorate with cream and blackberries.

HELEN'S HANDY CHOCOLATE OATCAKES

Serves as many as you can spare

Ingredients

200g/8oz margarine
150g/6oz sugar
200g/8oz rolled oats
25g/1oz cocoa
200g/8oz organic dark chocolate

When you're a student and your essays are doing your head in, take a break and make some of these. You'll be guaranteed instant friendship with a tray of them round the telly. They are quick, cheap and easy to make. Extra chocolate on top is optional but Helen knows what she'd recommend…

Melt the margarine.

Pile in the sugar, oats and cocoa and stir well.

Put into shallow baking tray.

Bake in a medium oven 180C°/gas mark 4 for 10–15 minutes

Cool in tin.

Coat with scrummy melted chocolate

To serve:

Cut into small squares so you can have seconds without too much guilt.

Make immediate appointment at local gym!

Pat's Diary

I haven't written a diary since school, but I've decided that this year I really should record everything that's happening. I only hope I've got time to keep it up.

JANUARY 2000

Kate Aldridge is in Morocco! What is she thinking of? Poor Phoebe, without her mum. I see Hayley's a victim of her good nature as usual, helping Roy out, bless her.

Jack and Peggy are back from their Guernsey hols with Lilian. Jack didn't think much of her latest toy boy. Apparently he's an actor. How does she find them?

Elizabeth's finding out what motherhood's all about now with Lily and Freddie. Good thing Jill's on hand. She's moved into Lower Loxley temporarily, although I gather Julia's been treating her a bit like the hired help.

FEBRUARY

Tommy's got a new girlfriend. That explains all those sightings of him with a mysterious blonde. Poor Kirsty. Hope he's let her down gently.

Eddie's tractor for sale in Borchester Echo.

check enough yog pots

BRIDGE FARM
Organic Yoghurt

Things must be bad, but Clarrie hasn't said a word to me. They'll pull through, as always.

Marjorie's second cataract operation has been done. Must be a relief to her.

Unexpected visit from tearful Hayley. She thought I'd be upset that she was seeing Roy, because of John. I was but not in the way she thought. I'm glad - and Roy's one of the best. Just feel sad at what might've been. She'd have made a great daughter-in-law.

Siobhan asked if we could sell her organic veg. Got me thinking. Whole ethos of organic is supplying locally and we're not doing that.

MARCH

Grange Farm bankrupt. Knew they sailed close to the wind but we thought they'd get by. Everything has to be sold to pay Borchester Land and other creditors. Why didn't Brian do something? My heart goes out to Clarrie.

Everyone in uproar at Brookfield. Phil and Jill want to hand over the farm to David and Ruth and find a new home, but Elizabeth is horrified - doesn't want to be done out of her share, it seems. Glad we don't have that sort of problem.

Shula's given up chocolate and made Alistair give up alcohol for Lent. Brave souls. If Tony had to give up Shires for 40 days, he'd be impossible to live with. Or should that be more impossible!

Hayley has plan to help Mrs A and Joe Grundy. Joe can help Marjorie get her confidence back driving again by going out in the car with her - and it'll keep him occupied. He's taken the bankruptcy very hard. Grange Farm was his life.

The Frys are back at Woodbine Cottage. Freda is thrilled with her new kitchen. Jill thought they were so happy in the bungalow they'd never want to leave.

Poachers have taken loads of trout from Brian's lake. Williams looking very worried. Doesn't bode well.

APRIL

He offered Helen the chance to run our new Borchester shop - and she said yes! Tony gave a lovely soppy speech at her 21st party. Made up a bit for his outrageous dancing. Tommy and Helen were mortified. Aren't parents embarrassing?

Helen's refused to sign David's Save The Grundys petition. Anything to help Clarrie, I say. So Tony and I put our names to it at once.

Clarrie's sold ~~Jethros~~ Jethro's old dresser to Lynda.

Row over who inherits Brookfield rumbles on. Twins christening ended in a huge row. Jill said she lost her temper, said she'd never been so ashamed. Kids.

Remind Tony re shopfitt

MAY

Brookfield sows got out into the lane near Hollowtree. David says they'll all be sold soon, no

clarrie re possible extra hours

money in pigs. Where does that leave Neil Carter?

He really surprised Debbie and Simon when they got married. They came out of the Register Office and there was Tony all ready with the tractor and trailer! He'd decorated them with lots of flowers and ribbons and I handed the happy couple glasses of champagne.

They laughed and climbed aboard and Tony drove them to the wedding breakfast at Grey Gables in true rural style. Pity Brian wasn't there. You'd have thought he could swallow his pride. Catastrophe when Phoebe sat on Jennifer's wedding hat. I had to get out the iron to steam it back into shape. Looked fine on the day.

Kathy and Sid don't seem to be getting on very well. All marriages go through rough patches, I suppose.

June

Tommy being very good helping set up the shop. Helen finishes college shortly, then can be with us full-time.

Poor Kathy's discovered that Sid has been having an affair – with Jolene Rogers. She's shattered. Doesn't know whether she can make a go of it with him, or even if ~~she wants two~~ she wants to.

Debbie really upset she can't rent Grange Farm. That weasel Matt Crawford insists its to be absorbed into Borchester Land.

Good that Siobhan has put up for the parish council. It'll do her good to have something else to think about. Time she joined the village properly.

Betty rang to say how well Roy had done in his exams. Good for him.

July

Joe's in hospital after going missing for a few days. He could have died. I get so angry about it. Eddie's determined to get them back to Ambridge somehow.

Lease for the shop to be completed on 17 July. Fingers and everything else crossed we make it a success. Helen certainly has some strong ideas about how it should be run.

Just heard Ruth has to have a breast removal. How awful! David's looking very worn.

Eddie's kept his promise – he and Joe very happily installed in a caravan – on estate land! Have to admire his cheek.

August

Social services have been to see Shula and Alistair several times about adopting Daniel.

Seems over the top. Bunty and Reg now reconciled to the idea.

Well, they tried, but there was just too much hurt. Kathy has left Sid and she and Jamie have moved in with us for the time being. Poor woman – 13 years down the drain.

Bit of staff trouble at the shop – I'm sure we'll sort it out.

September

Phew! We've been so busy I almost forgot about my diary.

Ruth spent last month recuperating after her op and is now starting chemotherapy. It's so awful for her.

On the brighter side, after a drawn-out process, Daniel's adoption has gone through, much to Shula's relief.

October

No doubt about it, despite how some regulars feel, Jolene is highly successful behind the bar at The Bull. He called in the other night and it was packed. They say there's no fool like an old fool. Well, there were quite a few young fools there too with their eyes on stalks and their tongues hanging out. Nothing like a 36DD to pull the punters.

Kathy is making the best of it, but it's hard for her, left out in the cold. I wonder what the future will bring for her?

fact file

NAME: JILL ARCHER née PATTERSON
BORN: 3 October 1930
ADDRESS: Brookfield Farm, Ambridge
OCCUPATION: Partner in Brookfield, beekeeper, hen feeder, unofficial child minder, ex-bed and breakfast proprietor, saint
FAMILY: Married to Phil. Two sons, Kenton and David, two daughters, Shula and Elizabeth. Five grandchildren, Pip, Josh, Daniel and twins Freddie and Lily
HOBBIES: Cake making, cooking and shopping, tea and sympathy
PAST SINS: Humiliated Lynda Snell in front of whole village, otherwise perfect!

Highs

1958 Twins Shula and Kenton born followed by David (1959) and Elizabeth (1967).
1988 Organised David and Ruth's wedding after Ruth's mother fell ill.
1993 Bakes brilliant orange and Cointreau madeira cake for granddaughter Pip's christening.
1999 Delighted to be a grandmother again.

Lows

1976 Collapses with a thyroid deficiency – myxoedema.
1991 Husband Phil leaves home after row over Jill's b&b guests.
1992 Daughter Elizabeth has an abortion without telling her mum.
2000 Daughter-in-law Ruth has a mastectomy.

What if...

Jill had another pair of hands
Or Jill hadn't been demonstrating that nifty kitchen device with 15 uses when she met Phil?

There can come a time in people's lives when everything suddenly goes haywire. For Jill Archer, one of Ambridge's best-loved villagers, the past 12 months have turned into her 'annus horribilis'.

When Jill injured her knee and couldn't manage stairs it made sense for the families to swap homes. David and Ruth and their children moved into the large farmhouse at Brookfield, while Jill and Phil took up residence in the bungalow.

It was not altogether a success. Jill and Phil found the bungalow cramped while Jill's bad knee meant she had to give up running her farmhouse bed and breakfast, a sideline she enjoyed. She almost sold her beloved bees, too, because it would be too much of a struggle to look after the hives, but Phil persuaded her to keep them.

Next, a lorry crashed into Woodbine Cottage, rendering tenants Bert and Freda Fry homeless and, as their landlord, it was up to Phil to find them accommodation. There was only one solution: Jill and Phil moved back into Brookfield alongside David and Ruth, leaving the bungalow free for the Frys.

Poor Jill. Two moves in a year and now squashed into her beloved Brookfield with her son, his wife and all the chaos that accompanies two small children.

They drew up rotas to share out the chores, but that didn't make for domestic bliss so they held a council of war. In a unanimous vote of confidence, Jill was elected best cook and she took charge of all the meals, much to everyone's relief. She did enjoy the increasing responsibility of looking after Pip and Josh, although she felt that Ruth wasn't always pleased with the results.

The arrival of Elizabeth's twins, Lily and Freddie, created even more work for Grandma Jill. She moved into Lower Loxley for a while to help with the night feeds as the twins' other grandmother, Julia Pargetter, proved to be a reluctant nappy-changer.

The Pargetters adored the babies but found them exhausting. Not only that but Lizzie herself had been born with a hole in the heart, and she needs a further operation. It is an anxious time for Jill.

But even anxieties about Elizabeth's health paled beside the row which erupted when Jill and Phil tried to plan their retirement. They had wanted to sell some of the farmland to David and Ruth to buy their retirement home. The mere idea of it sent shock waves of sibling rivalry through the children.

Elizabeth was outraged at the thought of 'losing' her inheritance, despite living in style at Lower Loxley. Shula thought her sister was being selfish but Kenton supported Elizabeth, despite having already received his share of the family wealth. David's attempts to find a compromise ended in blazing arguments with Phil. The situation dissolved amid personal recriminations and bickering among the children and Jill will never forget the terrible row that spoiled the twins' christening.

With problems like these, and poor Ruth needing so much love and support in getting over her breast cancer operation, life hasn't been easy this year. Not that Jill would admit it or fail to face up to it. One of the many good things you can say about Jill is that she's a fighter.

Patricia Greene

Patricia (known as Paddy) Greene had always intended to act, although her headmistress in Derby tried to dissuade her from following such a precarious career.

After the Central School of Speech and Drama in London, her aim was to be a classical actress but *Archers* producer Tony Shryane insisted she was perfect for the role of Phil Archer's new wife in 1957. Jill came from the town, didn't know what combine harvester meant or what grew on arable land, and was thus able to ask naive agricultural questions. Paddy fitted the bill.

Paddy has played Jill for nearly 44 years and in 1997 was awarded an MBE for services to radio.

In 1994 Paddy was one of the authors of the very successful *Book of The Archers*. She takes part in *Call My Bluff* and has appeared in *Casualty* and the BBC's daytime drama *Doctors*.

Her own 'real' life at home in a village in the Thames Valley includes reading, watching others gardening, dining with friends, going to the theatre and recording tapes for the visually impaired – a very Jill-like occupation.

YOU GOT THREE ROUNDS

One Pint – so easy a Grundy could do 'em.

Two Pints – maybe the Aldridges could get in a pint for once!

and

Three Pints – you'd 'ave to be an Archer or a Tucker to get these.

...AND WHAT DO PINTS MEAN?

We all likes a gossip, and being a milkman I 'as a bit of a laugh when doin' me rounds. You'd be surprised what people get up to early in the morning! I reckon I knows more than anyone about people who've lived round and about Ambridge, so I've 'ad a bit of fun and put together a quiz about The People Time's Forgot.

We all know Sid's got other things on his mind, so to speak, so this'll keep your 'and in until he gets round to the next Quiz Night at The Bull.

Anyways, here's a test of what you might have picked up as I expect you've done a bit of eavesdropping in your time.

The People Time's Forgot – One Pint Round

1. Who got put inside for organising an armed raid on the village shop?

2. What was the name of Jack Woolley's dog?

3. What is the name of Eddie Grundy's elder brother?

4. What was the name of Mrs Antrobus' favourite Afghan bitch?

5. What is the name of the chauffeur who drives the Bentley at Grey Gables?

6. Who took great pride in looking after the village telephone box?

7. Who very nearly got involved with Neil Carter while his wife Susan was in prison?

8. Who worked for Nelson Gabriel in the wine bar?

The People Time's Forgot – Two Pints Round

9. Who was the farmer who helped Neil Carter set up his pig business?

10. Who is responsible for most of the building and repair work around Ambridge?

11. Who was the policewoman who turned out to be Nelson Gabriel's daughter?

12. Who was the last Vicar of Ambridge, before it became part of the combined Amvale Parishes?

13. Who got Jennifer Archer into trouble?

14. Who thought they saw a ghost at Arkwright Hall – but it was only a gypsy?

15. What was the name of the Welshman who was Dan Archer's shepherd at Brookfield who married a girl called Mary?

16. Who was the mother of Jack Woolley's adopted daughter Hazel?

The People Time's Forgot – Three Pints Round

17. Who was the last headmistress of Ambridge Village School?

18. What are the names of Robert Snell's daughters by his previous marriage?

19. Apprenticed to Ben White, which Ambridge baker had been a ship's baker?

20. Who had a milk round, and drove her tractor with a fag in her mouth wearing a tea-cosy hat?

21. Whose ghost was supposed to haunt Martha Woodford?

22. Who was Nigel Pargetter's best friend who didn't become his best man?

23. Eddie Grundy was engaged to someone else before Clarrie. Who was it?

24. Who proposed to Carol Grey, was turned down by her but married her years later?

PINTS MEAN PRIZES!....................Now turn to page 96 to find out how clever you are!

Gardening Tips

Here are Bert Fry's tips for summer and autumn gardening, including a tasty recipe for marrow wine!

summer

Summer should be the time to sit down and enjoy the fruits of your labours. The trouble is, there's also so much to get done, and if you do sit down, you spots something that's demanding attention. I know Freda will be going around dead-heading the roses and I will do battle with the weeds, particularly in the vegetable plot. Keep your hoe clean and sharp for the best results.

Don't neglect your lawn either. It needs feeding just as much as cutting.

Then there's the soft fruit to be picked. Make sure you get your gooseberries and blackcurrants before the birds do. Some old net curtains thrown over the bushes will do the trick. Freda will be into her jam making any day now.

The biggest chore at this time of year is the watering. A couple of dry weeks, the garden looks parched and there's a hose pipe ban before you know it. Mr Archer tells me I need a licence to use a sprinkler, so I'm avoiding that one. We've got a huge old barrel I got off Sid Perks at The Bull. I fitted a tap to the bunghole, stood it on a pile of bricks and it fills in no time with rainwater from the guttering. Good clean water it is, with no added chemicals, and you can see my chrysanths and dahlias leaning out to meet it when I'm out with the watering can.

I hope you've been keeping your compost topped up, turned over and used in rotation. You'll need a ready supply for potting. Plants you keep permanently in pots will need re-potting one size up and those grown from seed will need potting on at intervals through the summer.

autumn

You'd be surprised how many plants that flowered in the spring and summer often bloom again in the fresher cooler weather.

Sweet peas can be planted in your greenhouse, and talking of which, don't forget to take off that whitewash you put on the roof in the summer. Any remaining green tomatoes in the greenhouse should be put in a drawer under some newspaper. They say you should always put a ripe one in with them to give them the idea of turning red. It may be an old wives' tale, but it's always worked with me.

There's a bit of digging to be done and preparation of seed beds. I always save a few old twigs and branches to keep the cats off. They think you've been preparing that seed bed for their own private use.

The big thing to remember now is getting the bulbs in for next spring. I always add a little bone meal a couple of weeks before planting, and make sure they goes well into the ground and have good drainage.

Hardy annuals can be sown now if you want them to flower next spring onwards. Apart from the more usual ones why not try some marigolds, larkspur or love-in-a-mist? Provided they're planted early they should be able to face up to the cold weather.

Something more restful? Have a look at the new seed catalogues. And why not take your missus for a drive to have a look at the autumn tints? Nothing like it at this time of year.

MARROW WINE

From a recipe first compiled in a Uri Dale farmhouse at the end of the 18th century.

Gather ye marrows. They must be firm and free of the mould. A goodly weight, at least 8lb each. Wash ye well their insides. Take ye a sharp knife and cut offe about four inches from the stalk end.

With a long-handled ladle remove ye the seeds, leaving softe fleshe inside. Finde a goode qualyte ladies silk hose, preferably without her in it. Cut offe ye big toe of hose and insert marrow within.

A hole should be made in ye marrow's nether end and ye whole hung from a hooke in ye larder. Place ye a bucket beneath it.

Ye marrow is now filled with dark raw sugar to its very top. Top up with sugar until there be no soft flesh left. Collect ye liquid and put in a large copper. Boil about ten minutes or one quarter inch length of candle.

Add a yeast from ye master's best French wine. Straine liquor into earthn jars and cork lightly for five days, then cork tightly and wire. Store in a cool place for four years.

Advance withe great care and open ye vessels withe not a shaky hand. Ye liquor to be treated withe great reverence, or woe to he who imbibes in quantity.

Not for the fainte hearted!

(Thanks to Frank Irwin, Ilkley for the recipe but Bert Fry and the authors take no responsibility for its consequences!)

MRS ANTROBUS PLAYS Santa Claus

When Mrs Antrobus decided to play Santa Claus to raise money for the church funds, it wasn't just the kids who wanted to sit on her knee and tell her what they wanted for Christmas. Parents came too…

MIKE TUCKER (below): A portable CD player with headphones to take on my milk round and drown out Phoebe on a bad day.

JOE GRUNDY: I'd like a couple of pints on the house afore I goes. Then I'd know there really was a Father Christmas.

PHOEBE ALDRIDGE: My mummy.

JULIA PARGETTER: A Christmas card from Nelson Gabriel.

WILLIAM GRUNDY: An honest dad.

MATT CRAWFORD: Another chance to get one over on Brian Aldridge.

LILY PARGETTER: We'd like Mummy to…

FREDDIE PARGETTER: …be happy all the time.

HAYLEY JORDAN (above): A little sparkly engagement ring would do me. Not that I want to rush things!

ELIZABETH PARGETTER: My birthright.

LAWRENCE LOVELL: To give the world my Lear.

PHIL ARCHER (above): A new home.

GREG TURNER: Just give me healthy game birds!

Reading between the lines

FACT OR FICTION? THE CHARACTERS IN *THE ARCHERS* ARE SO FAMILIAR TO US THAT WE FORGET THEY ARE PLAYED BY ACTORS. SO HOW MUCH OF THE ACTORS IS REVEALED IN THE CHARACTERS THEY PLAY?

TIM BEECHAM'S MATE HANDY ANDY (ANDREW PENNINGTON) HAS ANALYSED THE HANDWRITING OF THE FOLLOWING AMBRIDGE CONTRIBUTORS TO SEE HOW FAR CHARACTERS AND ACTORS OVERLAP. SEE WHAT YOU THINK...

ARCHES AND CURVES

ANGULAR LETTERS INDICATE DECISIVENESS

ARCHED LETTERS – 'ARCADES' – SUGGEST SOMEONE WHO CAN'T LET THEMSELVES GO

WHEN THE BOTTOM OF THE LETTERS CURVE LIKE A CUP – 'GARLANDS' – THE WRITER IS AT EASE WITH THEMSELVES AND THE WORLD AROUND THEM

WHEN THE WORDS ARE THREADED THE PERSON CONCERNED RELIES ON INSTINCT AND IS A RISK TAKER

SLANTS UP AND DOWN

BACKWARD SLANT INDICATES CAUTION, THOUGHTS AND ACTIONS BASED ON LOGIC

FORWARD SLANT SUGGESTS RESPONSIVENESS, EMOTIONAL INFLUENCE ON THOUGHTS AND ACTIONS

VERTICAL SLANT SHOWS A PERSON WHO CANNOT RELAX IN COMPANY AND DOES NOT FIT INTO A GROUP

VARIED SLANT SIGNIFIES A PERSONALITY THAT IS QUICK AND UNPREDICTABLE

LOOPS AND FIGURE EIGHTS

MISSING LETTERS, MISSING I DOTS AND T CROSSES SHOW ABSENT-MINDEDNESS

ENLARGED LOWER LOOPS SHOW A WARM DISPOSITION

BEWARE RIGID HANDWRITING WHICH WARNS OF ARROGANCE

FIGURE EIGHTS AND DISCONNECTIONS DEMONSTRATE CREATIVITY

REGULARITY AND PRECISION INDICATE PATIENCE

JACK WOOLLEY
ARNOLD PETERS

Jack Woolley is a self-made man of action with an ability to make money. He's run Grey Gables for years and is now enjoying a lively retirement, though still supervising Caroline Pemberton when it suits him. Could Arnold Peters do as well?

> Caroline,
> Now I know you're going to be cross, but Lynda looked so poorly I sent her home. We can't

The wide spacing and the positioning of his writing suggests that Arnold is full of vitality and courage, is well organised and gregarious. The use of the letter 'I' shows he is confident and likes to know where he is. The formulation of his capital letters tells us he is ambitious and likes to be as accurate as possible in all that he does. He is a spiritual and inspirational person. His lower case letters show that he is artistic and creative. He is sensitive to the opinion of others and good humoured, is always alert and thinks on his feet. A good chap to have at a party!

EDDIE GRUNDY
TREVOR HARRISON

Eddie Grundy is a born maverick who would have us believe he is also a born country and western singer. He can turn his hand to most farming chores but his chief ambition is to get rich quick with no effort on his part. His schemes are doomed to failure and his bankruptcy hit him hard. How is he going to get through the next year or so and could actor Trevor Harrison manage such difficulties in his own life?

computers but I can write a good letter as you can see. I'm reliable, conshienous, and will turn up every morning. Please get in touch.
Yours Sincerely
Eddie Grundy,

Trevor has a lot of willpower and intellectual energy and can stay controlled when the going gets tough. He is naturally diplomatic and is good with people, although he prefers to keep a personal distance when circumstances call for it. Although generally a calm person he can be energetic and forceful upon occasion. He is modest, instinctive and is quick to grasp opportunities as they arise. A loyal and non-judgmental friend and worthy of several pints of Shires in the local.

DAVID ARCHER
TIM BENTINCK

David Archer has a wife who knows nearly as much about farming as he does, and two children. He can't wait to run Brookfield Farm independently and is impatient of restraint. He has been extremely supportive of Ruth during her illness and irritated with his siblings over their wrangling about the future of Brookfield. Is Tim Bentinck David's twin?

As you know, farming has turned into a dicey business at best but we had a cancer scare with Ruth which really brought home to me just how precarious our existence is ...

Tim's handwriting suggests that he is self-confident and can occasionally be impatient. He is practical and ambitious and knows precisely what he wants out of life, and his confidence enables him to plan well for the future. Artistic, imaginative, creative – perhaps he enjoys a hobby such as landscape painting as his handwriting suggests that he enjoys being on his own for relaxation. Overall an intelligent, balanced and thoughtful person.

HAYLEY JORDAN
LUCY DAVIS

Hayley Jordan is one of the most popular young women in Ambridge. Kind and bubbly, she keeps an eye on Mrs Antrobus as well as all the children in her charge. Roy Tucker couldn't have done better in his choice of girlfriend and little Phoebe is flourishing in her care. But Hayley can more than hold her own. Can Lucy Davis?

Dear Roy
I've told Pat all about us and she doesn't mind a bit. It's such a relief and I don't feel so guilty about John now. In fact I think he'd be pleased, don't you?

The positioning of Lucy's perfectly upright handwriting suggests that she is an intelligent, self-controlled and balanced person. She is practical and likes to keep things in life plain, with a minimum of fuss – at the same time keeping her mind free and unhampered. Ambitious and confident with a strong will she likes to plan ahead and prefers to know what is waiting round the next corner. Although she is a calm personality she is also very energetic and doesn't pull her punches when the occasion calls for it. A good person to have on your side!

Birth OF AN INSTITUTION

When The Archers went nationwide in 1951, it was an instant success. Here we recall how the nation was prepared for life in Ambridge and, overleaf, meet the founding families of the village

AFTER ITS first nationwide broadcast at 11.45am on January 1 1951, *The Archers* was an instant success. The 'everyday story of country folk' attracted two million listeners, and by Easter had moved to 6.45pm, a peak listening slot. Within a week the audience had doubled.

Godfrey Baseley (above) had edited the programme for 22 years when he wrote: 'Perhaps the most important thing in *The Archers'* favour is that it is authentic, and behind us is every rural organisation of importance, ready to help in presenting a true picture of the countryside, and to bring a breath of fresh air every day to tired and weary townsfolk.'

Original producer Tony Shryane who produced the programme for 28 years was justly proud of the authentic sound effects: 'Recordings have been made at Women's Institute meetings, village churches, riding schools, parks and country estates, railway stations, farms, cattle markets and skittle alleys.'

Val Gielgud, head of radio drama in 1951, called it: 'Acceptable hokum'.

Whatever the reason, the programme continued to thrive and by the time it was 10 years old 11 million listeners were tuning in.

When *The Archers* went nationwide in 1951, series creator Godfrey Baseley produced a special programme to introduce the wider audience to the characters. He took a 'mobile recording vehicle' to meet the villagers of Ambridge, calling first at Brookfield Farm to meet Dan and Doris Archer, and their farm labourer, Simon Cooper. This is how it went:

SCENE ONE. BROOKFIELD EXTERIOR

DAN: Mr Baseley's coming down here to put us on the wireless.

SIMON: (UNIMPRESSED) Gaffer, I've finished that bit of grinding. Shall I go and stop that gap where the sheep got through?

DAN: (HEARTILY) Good idea, Simon.

SCENE TWO. BROOKFIELD INTERIOR

DORIS: Mr Baseley, would you like a cup of tea?

DAN: We're rare ones for tea here.

NARRATOR: After his tea Godfrey went to see reprobate farmer Walter Gabriel:

GODFREY: We are going to come down here regularly to hear what's going on at Mr Archer's farm and put it over on the wireless.

WALTER: (WHEEZING) Wireless. I don't hold with these new-fangled nonsenses.

NARRATOR: Godfrey then talked to Dan Archer's son, Phil, and Grace Fairbrother:

GODFREY: I've sort of bumped into a bit of romance, eh?

PHILIP: Oh no. No, not really.

GRACE: Just friends.

GODFREY: I found my way back to Brookfield Farm, chatted some more with Mrs Archer, made the final arrangements for the broadcast and, well, you'll hear all about that for yourselves if you listen to the *Light Programme* at a quarter to twelve on Monday the first of January. I do hope you enjoy eavesdropping on these country folk. Good night.

The very first episode of *The Archers* went out on January 1 1951 with a cast featuring Harry Oakes as Dan, Gwen Berryman as Doris, Norman Painting as Phil, Pamela Mant as Christine and Denis Folwell as Jack. Written by Geoffrey Webb and Edward J. Mason, edited by Godfrey Baseley and produced by Tony Shryane, it began with a message of good cheer to all those clustered around the wireless on that New Year's Day:

DAN: And a happy New Year to all.

DORIS: (QUIETLY) A very happy New Year, Dan.

DAN: Thanks mother. If it's as good as the last 'un I'll be satisfied.

JACK: How about some more of that rich and ripe old cooking port, Dad?

THE ARCHER FAMILY (above)
Holding up a mirror to farming
Britain in the 1950s

The Archer family (above) lived at Brookfield Farm. Dan Archer was a tenant farmer in his mid-fifties, struggling in that post-war austerity period to come to terms with changes both on the farm and in the countryside around Ambridge. His story reflected what was taking place all over Britain.

Dan had grown up in the days when Squire Lawson-Hope acted as both local landlord and lord of the manor. Dan's wife Doris (formerly Doris Forrest) had, like many young girls of her age, started work in service at the Manor, first as a kitchen maid and then as personal maid to the Squire's wife, Lettie.

They had been married for more than 30 years and had raised a family in that rambling farmhouse. Their elder son, Jack, was married to Peggy (née Perkins) with a family of his own. Disinclined to follow in his father's footsteps, he was content to run a smallholding.

Younger son Philip, on the other hand, had a natural talent for farming and was eager to introduce modern methods to Brookfield, even if it meant being at odds with his father.

To complete the family there was Christine, a typical farmer's daughter. At ease with the animals, always ready to lend a hand, keen on horses - her ambition was to run her own riding stables.

JACK ARCHER AND FAMILY
The wayward son who turned to drink

Jack Archer was uprooted from life on the farm to serve in the Army during the Second World War. By 1951 he had married Peggy, a pretty ATS girl from London, who settled with him in Ambridge. They had two daughters, Jennifer and Lilian, followed by a son, Tony.

Jack wasn't sure where he was going. He was never very happy doing the chores, such as washing the eggs ready for the customers. In 1952 he gave up the smallholding and went to live in Cornwall, but when that didn't work out the family returned to Ambridge.

During the day Jack worked for his father at Brookfield, and in the evenings began learning about the licensed trade, although some would say he was already too familiar with the subject. Eventually, he took over the tenancy of The Bull, which should have solved all his problems.

But he was soon restless, began drinking and gambling and was rude to the customers. He wasn't helped by the interfering presence of his mother-in-law, Mrs Perkins, known to all as Mrs P, who took no pains to hide what she thought of Jack.

Impatient at Jack's irresponsible management, the long-suffering brewery insisted that if the family wanted to stay at The Bull Peggy must become the licensee. It was the making of the family's fortunes. Under Peggy's iron rule The Bull prospered, but ironically it was the cause of Jack's undoing. Resentful of Peggy's success, he became an alcoholic and suffered severe depression, compounded by daughter Jennifer having an illegitimate baby in 1967. Despite treatment, Jack died in a clinic in 1972, at the age of 50.

After many years on her own Peggy married Jack Woolley and was able to close the book on that early part of her life.

THE GABRIELS
Like father, like son?

Walter Gabriel with his corncrake voice and highly individual approach to life was Ambridge's 'character', loved and endured by the villagers who never knew what to expect from him next.

Being almost the same age, he and Dan Archer would have been in the same class at Ambridge Village School. They were certainly the best of friends; Dan quietly accepting all of Walter's little eccentricities with a wry smile, but always willing to put his hand in his pocket to help Walter when he got into a scrape.

'Dan, me old pal, me old beauty,' was often heard emanating from Walter's mouth. Walter had a farm on the old Squire's estate, and received more than one warning about the way it was run. After he gave up farming he embarked on a series of unusual enterprises, each one losing more money than the last.

Walter's wife Annie died when their son Nelson was still quite young. Nelson Gabriel was the apple of his father's eye, but it wasn't until later in life that Nelson began to show some of the characteristics he had inherited. Nelson did his National Service in the RAF, and it must have been a great disappointment to Walter when he decided to sign on and not return to Ambridge for some years.

Despite their differences, the two Gabriels stood by and supported each other until Walter died in 1988. Not for the first time, Nelson's current whereabouts remain a mystery, although his creditors would dearly like to get in touch.

THE COOPER FAMILY
A farmworker's tale

The 1950s were times of great change in the farming industry as tractors replaced horses, the threshing machine gave way to the combine harvester and traditional skills were no longer required.

Nowhere was this more apparent than at Brookfield and for a worker like Simon Cooper who had spent all his life on a farm it must have been a difficult time.

But then Dan Archer was not one to bring in change too quickly and was always appreciative of Simon's work, even trying to persuade him to set up on his own. Simon was a gentle chap and the only time he lost his temper was when he mistakenly thought Dan suspected him of fiddling the books at the smallholding.

Simon always addressed Dan as 'gaffer' as befitted their different stations in life and was rarely without his hat.

Simon was happy in the tied cottage he shared with his wife Bess Cooper who came from a large family in Hollerton. Other than that, you'd find him in The Bull playing dominoes or skittles and trying to make a half of mild last the whole evening. He'd also be quietly goading his lifelong friend and drinking companion, Walter Gabriel. Simon would ask a question which would always be greeted with the same, age-old response from Walter: 'Well, my old Granny always used to say...'

In 1956 Simon had back trouble and had to retire, but Dan allowed the Coopers to stay on in their cottage until Simon died two years later. They had no children so Bess went to live with her sister.

THE CAREYS, MOTHER AND SON
Romance at the manor

Squire Lawson-Hope and his wife Lettie were at the centre of the Ambridge social life, and it was to their home at the Manor in 1951 that the recently-widowed Helen Carey came to stay with her son, Alan.

Alan Carey had served with a tank regiment in Korea, where he had been wounded and suffered severe depression after seeing his twin brother Rex burned alive. Essentially a countryman, he was fond of bird-watching and playing tennis and it was thought that staying at the Manor might help him to recover.

Helen was an old friend of the Lawson-Hopes and they did all they could to introduce her to 'the right sort of people' in Ambridge. This included the former businessman George Fairbrother, a widower who had recently bought a farm and settled in Ambridge with his daughter, Grace.

Of course the inevitable happened. Grace was drawn to this brooding young Army officer, and helped him back to normality. Alan proposed to Grace, but when she turned him down his depression returned. Soon after, on a visit to Yorkshire, he met the attractive Ann Fraser and they fell in love. This time his proposal of marriage was accepted and the couple made their home in Yorkshire.

Cupid's arrow was not confined to the younger generation. Helen Carey was still only 42 when she met George Fairbrother, and although she admitted to being apprehensive about taking on Grace as a step-daughter, she graciously accepted George's offer of marriage and moved into his farmhouse.

REGGIE AND VALERIE TRENTHAM
A match made in Grey Gables

'Man about town meets femme fatale' is how the *Borchester Echo* would have described the arrival of Reggie Trentham with Valerie Grayson on his arm in 1952.

Everyone in Ambridge knew Reggie Trentham and took him as they found him. He was a bit of a rogue, fond of riding and boxing, and no mean bowler on the cricket field, as his record with Ambridge Cricket Club shows.

Reggie was a director of Grey Gables Country Club, and all Ambridge smiled wryly when he installed Valerie as a club hostess. So began a long and tempestuous courtship with Valerie finally agreeing to marry Reggie. Three years later their daughter Hazel was born.

Reggie Trentham died, not in Ambridge, but abroad, in the Bahamas. By this time Grey Gables had been sold to Jack Woolley. Jack wanted to go off on a cruise and was delighted when Valerie Trentham returned and offered to run Grey Gables in his absence.

Valerie, 'the merry widow', eventually became Mrs Jack Woolley, but she showed little interest in Jack or in their new home. Once Hazel was away at boarding school Valerie embarked on a series of affairs, and then disappeared from

CLOCKWISE FROM TOP LEFT: Walter Gabriel (Chriss Gittins) 1961; Walter (left) with Simon Cooper (Eddie Robinson) 1957; Nelson Gabriel (Jack May) 1992; Peggy (June Spencer) and Jack Archer (Denis Folwell), 1951

Ambridge. She did ensure that Jack legally adopted Hazel, a move that delighted Jack but had little effect on the daughter.

Jack blamed himself when Valerie died of drink, but those who had lived longer in Ambridge remembered the days of Reggie and Valerie Trentham and knew better.

THE FAIRBROTHERS
Grace, darling

The arrival of George Fairbrother and his daughter Grace in 1951 was to have a profound influence on events in the village. Why did Fairbrother move to Ambridge and buy a small farm after he had made a fortune in plastics? Was it to move away from memories of his late wife or was it to indulge his daughter Grace with her love for horses and everything to do with the social life in the country?

It was when he was fishing one day in his trout stream that George realised that he had fallen for the charms of Helen Carey, a widow staying with Squire Lawson-Hope. After a short courtship they were married.

At first Grace didn't take kindly to her father's re-marriage, perhaps because she had to take second place in his affections. However, Helen was a sensible woman of the world and used her calm persuasion to make Grace her friend as well as her step-daughter. The following year Helen gave birth to a son, Robin.

George Fairbrother was still very much a businessman at heart and enlarged his estate and brought in many modern farming methods that other farmers in Ambridge sneered at. The crunch came with the discovery of ironstone on the Fairbrother land. George aimed to mine the valuable ore and it was only after the intervention of Squire Lawson-Hope that George accepted that mining would bring devastation to the village.

He had several minor skirmishes with others in the neighbourhood, and it was usually left to Helen to smooth the ruffled feathers.

When Grace wanted to start a riding school George advised against it, but then relented and gave it his support. He didn't exactly encourage Grace in her pursuit of Phil Archer, but saw him for the sensible young farmer that he was and eventually made him a director and included him in his long-term plans.

Helen was a great comfort to George when Grace died. She persuaded him that life had to go on, but the death left such a deep impression that George sold up and the family moved away. It was left to Helen to return to make the arrangements for the memorial window to Grace in St Stephen's.

1951

THAT WAS THE YEAR THAT WAS

In 1951, Britain was still feeling the effects of post-war austerity. Food, clothing and petrol were on ration. The balance of payments and the dollar crisis were always in the news.

Out of the gloom came the Festival of Britain – and on to the BBC Light Programme came *The Archers*.

SEARCH CONTINUES FOR MISSING Submarine HMS AFFRAY

GENERAL MACARTHUR SACKED!

QUEEN MARY VISITS FESTIVAL OF BRITAIN

Dec. 30, 'Queen Mary' makes two ...mpton to sunny Las Palmas. ...sengers will

Ivor Novello Dies

Stone of Scone Returned to Westminster Abbey

Death of Ernest Bevin

HARLOW NEW TOWN OPENED

Ceasefire in Korea

Venice Floods!

Women Petition against 8d Meat Ration

Trouble in Suez Canal Zone

Israeli Prime Minister David Ben Gurion meets Albert Einstein

Churchill Returns to Number 10

AUSTRALIA CELEBRATES JUBILEE

Volcano erupts in Philippines

BBC Light Programme Presents The Archers 1 January 1951

Britain's New Fighter F1-11 - Test Flight

Oxford Boat Sinks

KOREAN WAR CONTINUES

Princess Elizabeth on Holiday in Mediterranean

Festival of Britain Opens

Royal Festival Hall Opens

Fatherkn ws

It's the Ambridge wedding of the year! Debbie Aldridge is the blushing bride and Canadian Simon Gerrard her dashing groom

Debbie met Simon when she was a student at Exeter University in 1991. He was a visiting lecturer from Canada and his confidence and charm attracted her from the start. She fell blissfully in love and, flattered by her admiration, he was happy to teach her much more than the French studies on the curriculum. Following her to Ambridge, he begged her to go back to Canada but she was too young to commit. He became angry and disappeared, telling her vaguely there was 'someone else'.

Broken-hearted, she never returned to Exeter to finish her studies.

However, all good fairy stories need a happy ending and after trials and tribulations the Prince claimed his Princess, although in this case it was some years before the lovers were re-united. Simon got a job at Felpersham University, insisted on meeting Debbie to explain why he had behaved as he had and once again worked his magic. When he wooed her this time he claimed that none of the other women in his life had matched up to what he felt for her.

Overcoming all Debbie's objections he persuaded her to live with him and when he went down on one knee to propose, starry-eyed she said yes.

BRIAN ALDRIDGE – WICKED BARON OR FAIRY GODFATHER?

Will they live happily ever after? Not according to Brian. He regards 'Slimon' as a frog rather than a prince. Only time will tell if he is the Wicked Baron, creating problems for the couple out of his jealousy and irrational dislike or the Fairy Godfather, trying to ensure the happiness of his much loved step-daughter. His absence from the wedding ceremony spoke volumes. He made it plain that the event took place without his blessing but Debbie should have been grateful he didn't cast a bad spell over the proceedings. Certainly, Brian would happily have made Simon disappear in a puff of smoke.

So when Debbie Aldridge became Mrs Simon Gerrard, Brian, her step-father, friend and ally, was missing from the happy throng. He took himself out of Borsetshire for a few days 'on business' and even refused to help Jennifer by looking after his granddaughter Phoebe.

It's as if he can't accept that his little girl has finally grown up, and Debbie is at a loss to know how to handle him.

Matters weren't helped prior to

best?

the wedding when Brian found out that Simon had been suspended from work. A female student alleged that Simon had sexually harassed her, and Brian's worst fears were confirmed. Even when Simon was reinstated after the girl withdrew her allegations. Brian was still suspicious, alternately raging and pleading with Debbie, begging her to see sense. That of course made her cling to Simon all the more.

There was further friction when Brian learned of Debbie and Simon's interest in renting Grange Farm after the eviction of the Grundys. Anxious to avert another row, Debbie hadn't told Brian when she went to consult Graham Ryder but Ambridge is a small village. But Matt Crawford was more than happy to pass on the news to Brian and enjoy his humiliation, and soon Debbie was in the middle of the very row she had hoped to avoid!

Debbie spent the night before the wedding with her mother and sister Alice at Home Farm. She was hurt and sad that Brian wasn't there, but when she went to her room after dinner, she found he had left her a charming necklace on her dressing table, with a note: 'Love, Dad'.

DO YOU, DEBORAH ALDRIDGE, TAKE THIS MAN...?

Debbie and Simon were married at Borchester Register Office. Alice was the ring-bearer and looked smart and important in the special new dress Simon and Debbie bought her for the occasion. Little Phoebe was in a new dress too, which cunningly matched Jennifer's ensemble. Jennifer's elaborate hat looked as good as new despite having been

accidentally flattened by Phoebe! Undaunted. Jennifer worked wonders steaming it back into shape in time.

Only close family and friends were invited. The Woolleys and Nigel and Elizabeth Pargetter were happy to attend. However, Brian was not the only member of the family conspicuously absent from the feast.

Debbie particularly missed the abrasive comments of her younger sister Kate, still roaming around Africa 'finding herself', and her elder step-brother, Adam Macy, who hasn't been home for years, preferring to live and work in the developing world. Jennifer had hoped they'd fly back for the wedding, but without success. Kate couldn't be tracked down; Adam was too busy but sent his warmest wishes for a happy life to them both.

It was a lovely spring day. The wedding went without a hitch with Elizabeth as one witness and 'Bondi' Blanchard, an academic friend of Simon's, as the second. When they came out of the Register Office into the sunlight, the happy couple were surprised by Pat Archer with two glasses of champagne.

Not only that, but Tony Archer was waiting, dressed in Higgs' chauffeur uniform, at the wheel of a decorated tractor and trailer, bedecked in flowers and streamers. Simon and Debbie climbed aboard for the ride to their wedding breakfast at Grey Gables.

After their wonderful day Mr and Mrs Simon Gerrard spent a short honeymoon in Paris, saving their main holiday for the summer when they visited Simon's family and friends in Canada.

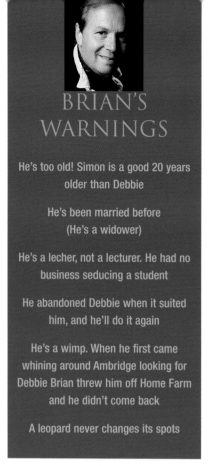

BRIAN'S WARNINGS

He's too old! Simon is a good 20 years older than Debbie

He's been married before (He's a widower)

He's a lecher, not a lecturer. He had no business seducing a student

He abandoned Debbie when it suited him, and he'll do it again

He's a wimp. When he first came whining around Ambridge looking for Debbie Brian threw him off Home Farm and he didn't come back

A leopard never changes its spots

When Brian got home Jennifer told him how well the wedding had gone and how much she had missed his not being there. 'It reminded me of our own wedding,' she told him, with a touch of wistfulness.

Now it's all over, Jennifer feels sad about the day. Brian won't even be in the photos. He too is sad about the whole affair, unhappy it turned out this way. He had left Debbie his gift but he knew really that the best present he could have given her would have been to be there in person to see her marry Simon.

With the wedding and honeymoon over Debbie and Simon are keen to get on with their life together but it's unlikely to be as simple as that. Borchester Land kept them in suspense over Grange Farm before deciding against offering them the tenancy.

Meanwhile Brian's dislike of Simon keeps the family rift alive. Will he be proved right about his loathed son-in-law? And if so, will it bring him much satisfaction?

Dr CHARLES YOUNG: Lynda, you were unanimously elected by the selection committee in Ambridge to come on the Psychiatrist's Couch. Why do you think that was?

LYNDA: Such a compliment. I agree with them. I am the perfect choice.

CHARLES: And why is that?

LYNDA: They must have realised that there would be a meeting of minds, and they know from their own experience just how much I can help you.

CHARLES: I see. Now let's start at the beginning. You were born in May, 1947?

LYNDA: Yes indeed – I'm a pig.

CHARLES: Not at all. You only had a couple of biscuits.

LYNDA: No, I mean pig as in boar. I am a boar.

CHARLES: It's odd you should say that because...

LYNDA: It was a bit of a blow when I found out. A dog would be much more in my style. Something aristocratic and elegant – a greyhound perhaps or a pointer. When were you born?

CHARLES: Oh, um, April 12.

LYNDA: What year?

CHARLES: 1948.

LYNDA: You're a rat.

CHARLES: That's a bit harsh!

LYNDA: Figuratively speaking of course. Have you ever dreamed of rats or ever felt yourself drawn to one?

CHARLES: No.

LYNDA: How odd. Sometimes we feel an affinity with our animal – although I must admit I'd never been keen on pigs, such grunty things. However, I'm told they are very intelligent.

CHARLES: We seem to be wandering from the point

LYNDA: On the contrary Charles, this is very much to the point. Until you know your animal you can't start to sort out where you should live or for that matter who you should live with.

CHARLES: I'm sorry?

LYNDA: You mean you've never heard of feng shui? My dear Charles, it will change your life. It's a very ancient Chinese method of controlling cosmic energy – the ch'i – to our advantage. You work out what animal you are from your year of birth and everything else stems from that. Someone in your position should know all about it if you really want to help your patients.

CHARLES: I don't think my lack of knowledge about the workings of feng shui has affected my patients badly.

LYNDA: Of course you don't. That's because you're blocked. Poor Anthony, all that negative ch'i just aching to get out. Thank goodness I came along today – I only hope I'm in time.

CHARLES: Er, Lynda, we are supposed to be talking about you

LYNDA: That's absolutely fine Charles, don't mind me. I'll just rearrange a few things while we talk and you'll be amazed at the difference it'll make. Robert certainly was.

CHARLES: Ah, that's your husband, Robert. I understand that he's been married before and that there are two children by his first marriage. Has this caused difficulties?

LYNDA: Of course. They're completely yan and ying. They should complement each other but it's not as easy as that I'm afraid. Can you help me move this chair?

CHARLES: What are you going to do with it?

LYNDA: It'll be much better over there. And if you don't mind my saying so you could do with some more pot plants. I'll just get rid of these flowers. Avoid cut flowers whenever you can. It's bad ch'i.

CHARLES: Right. May I sit down again, now?

LYNDA: Of course. If you turn your head round you can still see me. Now where were we?

CHARLES: I know you've lived in Ambridge for the past 15 years or so but you are probably still considered a newcomer. Are you accepted in the village?

LYNDA: Oh, yes, absolutely. To be honest I don't know how they managed before I came along. They ask me to organise all the big events and local drama, you know. I try to get out of it each year but I have to take pity on them – or nothing would ever happen.

CHARLES: And you also have a job?

LYNDA: Yes, I assist Caroline Pemberton at Grey Gables luxury hotel. I do my little best to improve things there. I've tried to attract wealth with my wind chimes, not that I've been shown any gratitude. Caroline was quite rude when I explained that we should paint the walls red.

CHARLES: Why was that?

LYNDA: Her age probably.

CHARLES: I meant, why should she paint the walls red?

LYNDA: It's another way of attracting wealth. I know the hotel does very well but there's always room for improvement.

CHARLES: Would you say that you prefer being a big fish in a small pool, or a small fish in a big pool?

LYNDA: What a very interesting question…I wonder what brought it to your mind?

CHARLES: Is there an answer?

LYNDA: Well, obviously it would be better to be in a small pool as too much ch'i would accumulate in a big one and that wouldn't do at all.

CHARLES: A big fish then. And how does Robert feel about that?

LYNDA: I don't know what Robert feels about anything at the moment. He's being astonishingly intolerant but I'm sure we'll sort it out. I think most of our problems are based on the fact that our house is pointing in the wrong direction. We may have to move.

CHARLES: Are you normally a confident person?

LYNDA: Well, I've been blessed you know. I have wonderful friends who appreciate all that I do for them. I'm much respected where I live. I'm very fulfilled in my work and I'm having an impact on my environment wherever I go. So I have a great deal to be confident about, don't I?

CHARLES: Yes indeed.

LYNDA: Well now Charles I mustn't keep you. It's after one o'clock so you'll be past your best.

CHARLES: Any particular reason?

LYNDA: Oh, you can't help it. It's just that rats are at their most decisive between eleven and one and it's getting on for two. So I expect you'd like a little rest now.

CHARLES: I could certainly do with a lie down. Thank you and goodbye Lynda.

KITCHEN GARDEN

TREE TOP WALK

Hello everyone. I hope you have a jolly good time as you make your way round the Lower Loxley Oddity Trail. It's for children of all ages. I've dotted some everyday articles in some weird places for you to find. And I've put together some fiendishly cryptic clues to help you discover them. Good luck!

To get you started – can you find the answer to clue no. 1? It's a b****a.

Turn the page upside down to find the answers to the rest.

clues

1. Did King Charles II peel one where he hid?

2. Jumping from tree to tree on high is where you would expect to find me.

3. Most kitchens have the time, but not with the bird.

4. If you don't see him first he'll see you later, in the water.

5. People think I'm quackers because I'm orange.

6. Surely these apples grow on pine trees?

7. You'd usually see this in the nursery, not the folly.

8. If you called our female relatives this there would be a massacre!

9. It is cold enough for it, but not in see-through France.

10. Where the Pargetters might have found two little ones, looking alike.

New Voices

EDWARD GRUNDY

Eddie and Clarrie's younger son, the hormonally-challenged teenager, played by **BARRY FARRIMOND**

Edward Grundy – Ed to his mates – is a beer-swilling, rather unlovable 16-year-old who smokes on the buses and carries a torch for Emma Carter, which isn't reciprocated, though they are friends. When not out vandalising churches, he spends hours by himself, drowning out his mother's inquiries with very loud music. Older generations irritate him, especially when they snore, and he wants to leave home like his elder brother.

Yes – Ed is a teenager all right and 19-year-old Barry Farrimond is relishing the role. 'We are fairly similar types. I can remember being a bit wild when I was at school,' he says, 'though my voice sounded like a cat on fire.' Barry thinks Edward lost his good singing voice when his voice broke.

There have been good stories for Barry since his arrival, such as Edward's frustration at having to share a room with his snoring grandad Joe and his craving for privacy which drove him to build a pseudo bed-sit in the living room at Meadow Rise. And it was Edward who revealed Sid and Jolene's affair – 'I know it's true, Fallon said,' he told his mother.

Barry has wanted to act since he was six after a speech therapist recommended acting to help him overcome problems with 'th' sounds. 'I think it was because I was an extrovert – laughing all the time and running around like a mad thing,' he says. 'But it did the trick and I can now say thank you properly.'

His credentials are good and he's already worked with some of the great names in English theatre. He attended the Sylvia Young Theatre School in London and went on to study Performing Arts at Stratford College. He lives in Stratford-upon-Avon where his first acting role at 11 was the son of Olympia with Anthony Sher in *Tamburlaine the Great* at the Royal Shakespeare Theatre. He went on to play Fleance in the Derek Jacobi RSC production of *Macbeth* and worked on Ted Hughes' adaptation of Frank Wedekind's *Spring Awakening*, also for the RSC.

But radio is much harder and a greater challenge, Barry reckons. He enjoys having to put more expression in his voice and the fact that both the actors and the radio audience are using more of their imagination. Although he's not a long-standing listener, Barry finds *The Archers* gets more and more intriguing. 'I'm getting addicted. The cast are fantastic, and I get on with Philip Molloy (Edward's brother, William) and Felicity Jones (Emma Carter) just fine.'

Of course, Ed would hate it all.

LEWIS

The once-silent architect at Lower Loxley is brought to life by **ROBERT LISTER**

Like Inspector Morse's sidekick, we only know him as 'Lewis'. It's Lewis that the Pargetter family turned to for advice during all the work involved in constructing a cafe in the Orangery and converting the stable block into a souvenir shop at Lower Loxley, to say nothing of the deathwatch beetle, and his help with the twins.

For Nigel and Elizabeth it's been good to have professional help around when problems arise, and for Julia, well another man about the house is always welcome.

Such is the esteem in which Lewis's work is held that he was also commissioned to advise on the restoration of nearly-derelict Arkwright Hall, once a building of some splendour, which had been allowed to fall into disrepair.

Taking on the role of 'a new man in the village' is actor Robert Lister who lists 'things architectural and a love of antiques' among his interests.

Robert lives with his wife, Pat Friday, in Stratford-upon-Avon, and since radio has long been his favourite medium he was delighted when his neighbour Malcolm McKee (who plays Graham Ryder) advised him to audition for the part of Lewis.

He was no stranger to the *Archers* cast, having already worked with Graham Seed (Nigel) and Sara Coward (Caroline). He also met Patricia Gallimore (Pat) when her daughter attended his wife's theatre studies class.

Playing Lewis has meant scenes with Mary Wimbush (Julia Pargetter). He was, he says, overawed and overwhelmed by working with Mary, an actress he had admired for many years.

Apart from being involved with *The Archers* Robert has been on an educational tour, helping to bring historical characters to life for youngsters in Newcastle, Plymouth and Cardiff who are embarking on GCSEs. In *Hitler on Trial* Robert played Hitler's defence counsel, and he also appeared in several guises in *The Doctor's Show*.

After many months as a 'silent character' giving advice on deathwatch beetle, he's glad that at last Lewis has come out of the woodwork.

EMMA CARTER

Emma Carter, the teenage daughter of Neil and Susan Carter, is played by **FELICITY JONES**

Felicity Jones played baddie Ethel Hallow in the children's TV series *The Worst Witch*, so her mutinous streak was well honed by the time she was cast as Emma Carter, one of Ambridge's latest brat pack. Sixteen-year-old Felicity was spotted by *Archers* producer Julie Beckett at Carlton's Junior Television Workshop in Birmingham and she landed the role after a second audition in the BBC drama studio at Pebble Mill, which meant recording a scene with Susan (Charlotte Martin).

The new Emma Carter was first heard in an episode broadcast in April when her friend 'Ed' (Edward) Grundy was stuck on the church roof. Felicity says she will always remember those first lines: 'Are you trying to knock that over? Weren't the gravestones enough for yer?' in what she hoped was a convincing country voice. Although she claims to be a fairly good mimic this was the first time Felicity had used an accent in a part, and she was nervous.

Felicity was briefed to play Emma as a rebellious and insecure teenager, who wet the bed as a child and whose mother had been in prison. Besides being the same age as Emma, both also sat their GCSEs last summer and these things helped Felicity get under the skin of the part, she says. Coincidentally, she'd begun listening to the programme a month before the audition arose, so she had some background knowledge.

Although there are no showbiz family connections – her mum is in marketing and her dad works for an Internet company – Felicity has been acting since she joined Carlton Workshop at 11. She's also appeared in the film of E. Nesbit's *The Treasure Seekers*, and her first radio role was in the radio education series *What A Drag* but next on her agenda is A levels and, she hopes, university. Career plans can wait.

BRENDA TUCKER

Presenting **AMY SHINDLER** *as the fledgling radio star*

Amy Shindler plays Brenda, the singleminded teenage daughter of milkman Mike and shop manager Betty Tucker. Brenda decided against going to university to join the media. A fast learner, she's done well since she went to Radio Borsetshire, answering listeners calls, preparing interviews and making herself indispensable to presenter Wayne Foley. Her aim is to land a programme of her own.

Actress Amy Shindler would like the confident Brenda to turn into a bit of a bad girl, making her more of a challenge to play, but there's not too much sign of that so far!

Amy is half-American and the daughter of writer and producer Colin Shindler, who plays cricket

with Graham Seed (Nigel Pargetter). She trained with the Anna Scher Theatre for seven years, gained a History BA (Hons) degree with exhibition at Cambridge, and graduated in 1998 from the Webber Douglas Academy of Dramatic Art. She has been appearing on stage since she was six and last autumn played the saint-like Shelly in the BBC Choice production of *Sisters*.

Amy speaks German, French and Italian and has a fine soprano voice. She plays the piano and violin to grade 6 standard and has studied flamenco and Middle Eastern dance.

There is no end to her talents, as we shall discover.

50 Golden

Fifty people aged eight to 88 who have listened over the years, tell us what it is that they like about *The Archers*. They range from school children to lorry drivers, from social workers to civil servants:

1 It's good to hear other people's problems and not be part of them.
   Ralph Kennedy, Sunderland

2 They've become part of my life. I couldn't be without it.
   Angela Good, Richmond, Surrey

3 Much better than the television. You can see it all in your mind.
   Helen Boyle, Linton, Devon

4 It takes me back to my childhood when I was evacuated to the country during the war.
   Muriel Cohen, Stepney Green, London

5 My mother used to listen and I hated it. Now it's just grown on me.
   Joy Worth, Wraysbury

6 Makes me glad I live in London and don't have to put up with all their squabbles.
   Rupert Cave, London

7 Is it accurate? I like to think it is.
   Alan Stevens, Bristol

8 That stupid Sid annoys me. Fancy falling for someone as obvious as Jolene.
   June Jenkins, Malvern, Worcs

9 We have a farm and find we're up against many of the same difficulties. We're not as bad as the Grundys though.
   Mr and Mrs Graham Lovett, Castle Carey

10 Our twins are the same age as Lizzie and Nigel's and we like to compare their progress.
    Peter and Penny Jeffrey, Newmarket

11 I listen when I can because it helps me with my English study.
    Hans van der Werf, Amsterdam

12 When you get old, it's nice to have something to talk to other people about.
    S Catriona MacGregor (Miss), Chelsea, south-west London

13 Now and again it jogs my memory about what I ought to be doing on the farm.
    Mr Pardoe, Cumbria

14 I always thought it was for oldies, but now it's got some good young people.
    Rachel Parker, Dudley

15 All the characters seem so real to me. I feel they're my friends.
    Zoe Brebine (aged eight), New Mills, Derbyshire

16 I do feel that *The Archers* does convey the 'better' side of British life.
    Lilian Pound, Wolverhampton

17 The BBC will go straight to heaven for giving us *The Archers*.
    Billy Connolly

18 It seems to understand about life in the country far better than the politicians do.
    Mr and Mrs D Meadows, Stoke Farm, Gloucestershire

19 Warm, friendly, what I want to hear about – it's *The Archers*.
    Ms Jill James, Exeter, Devon

20 I'm always driving home at seven in the evenings, and it helps the last part of my journey go much more quickly.
    Roy Hammett, Henley-on-Thames

21 At least it has a view on ecology and the environment.
    Robin Lawrence, Salford

22 My sister sends me out tapes each week, which I love even though it makes me homesick.
    Helen Owen, Wellington, New Zealand

23 When my father was alive we had to be silent when it was on. Now it's my children who are the avid listeners.
    Peter Gilbert, Lewisham

24 I suppose it's how every city dweller like me has this rosy image of life in the country.
    Lesley Fraser, Birmingham

25 I shall never forget the night Grace was killed in the fire. We couldn't believe it, we were all in tears.
    Marjorie Kennedy, Belfast

26 I didn't listen for about ten years when I had the children, but when I started again it was like coming back home.
    Norma Raymond, Dover

27 A lot of my old favourites have gone – *Down Your Way, Children's Hour, Mrs Dale's Diary, Listen with Mother* – but *The Archers* is still there.
    Victoria J Wood, Anglesey

28 Sunday mornings wouldn't be the same without it. We have a pot of tea in bed and listen for a blissful hour and a quarter.
    Reg and Georgette Silver, Didsbury, Manchester

29 When I first came to Britain I couldn't understand a word of it – but now I have to have my daily fix of *The Archers*.
Paula Rutherford-Wright, Oxford

30 If ever there's a vacancy at St Stephen's I shall apply – even if it does mean looking after three parishes!
Rev Rolly Todd, Lanarkshire

31 All the men sound so cuddly with the exception of Brian. He's my pet hate.
Pauline Martin, Leeds

32 I get so cross with them at times. It's hard to realise that they are only acting a part.
Rebecca Richardson, Coventry

33 I used to live in Suffolk near a village called Grundisburgh. Could this be the ancient fiefdom of the Grundy family?
Mr M Smith, Norwich

34 Why oh why didn't I start listening years and years ago – the best thing on the radio. Why can't it be half an hour a day!
Mr T Jewell, Braunton

35 I am a pub landlord and I like going to the gym. THANKS A LOT, SID.
Mr G Thompson, Hexham

36 I cried buckets when Mark died, and cried more buckets when Alastair finally asked Shula to marry him, with lots of smaller buckets in between. Thank you writers and cast for allowing me to be part of your lives.
Mrs S Wysome, Yelverton

37 Am I the only one who goes 'Ahhh' whenever there's a scene with Roy and Hayley. Just one other thing - when can I be in it!
Miss B Spiteri, Stroud

38 I have two passions in life, apart from my family, one is the history of the *Titanic*, and the other *The Archers*.
Miss V Passmore, Exeter

39 Now that I'm a mother of two small children the programme is my oasis of calm during hectic days.
Mrs A Sabatani, USA

40 Beats *EastEnders* any day.
Mr L Bartlett, Bolton

41 Ever since Clive Horrobin first appeared on the scene there has always been one character who would be better off in prison. Elizabeth is my current favourite contender!
Andy Sharp, Newcastle

42 In about 1975 I saw a sketch on television in a programme dedicated to what life would be like in the year 2000. One of the scenes depicted a space mission returning from Mars and trying to raise ground control on the radio. They were flicking the dial round, trying to get the correct frequency, when suddenly the inimitable strains of *Barwick Green* came over the loudspeaker. Everybody laughed.
Frank Cross, London

43 I'm nearly 16, and my mum and I both keep up with *The Archers*. Brian – why doesn't someone do something really, REALLY horrible to him?
Miss C Plant, Gloucester

44 Thanks for the plot-lines in particular – there's much I miss about home, but I find to my surprise that I miss nothing nearly so much as the daily reference point that Ambridge provided.
Mr J Chapman, Sydney

45 I am surprised how many young people listen to *The Archers*! It is great being able to listen over the net.
Mr R Porter, Orlando

46 I have listened to *The Archers* since 1980 and only missed two episodes in that time. I don't have TV and enjoy the radio very much. Apparently my great grandmother was also an *Archers* addict.
Mrs C Loch, South Lanarkshire

47 I have admired David Archer from afar since I started listening, and he is even better looking than I thought!
Miss A Marsh, Tooting, South London

48 Every night I have to record it for my husband – I listen when I'm ironing!
Mrs P Firman, Bordon

49 I confess to being an *Archers* addict. I listen regularly but half of the characters get on my nerves, apart from Lynda Snell who is probably the only one who is supposed to.
Mr A Davies, Wirral

50 Got the 2000 annual for Christmas. Very informative. Hope this will be a regular thing!
Mrs K Usher, Taunton

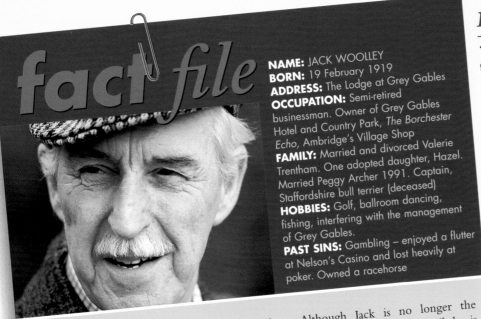

fact file

NAME: JACK WOOLLEY
BORN: 19 February 1919
ADDRESS: The Lodge at Grey Gables
OCCUPATION: Semi-retired businessman. Owner of Grey Gables Hotel and Country Park, *The Borchester Echo*, Ambridge's Village Shop
FAMILY: Married and divorced Valerie Trentham. One adopted daughter, Hazel. Married Peggy Archer 1991. Captain, Staffordshire bull terrier (deceased)
HOBBIES: Golf, ballroom dancing, fishing, interfering with the management of Grey Gables.
PAST SINS: Gambling – enjoyed a flutter at Nelson's Casino and lost heavily at poker. Owned a racehorse

Highs

1984 Grey Gables restaurant wins gourmet award, The Golden Rosette.
1984 Princess Margaret and Duke of Westminster visit Grey Gables.
1991 Wrests Peggy from Godfrey Wendover's arms, marries her and commissions a flower for her – the Ambridge Rose.
2000 Enjoys more free time now that he has passed on the running of Grey Gables.

Lows

1974 Suffers first heart attack on hearing Valerie is suing him for divorce.
1991 Returns from honeymoon to find his dog Captain is dead.
1993 In hospital again after collapsing in shock at the shop when raider Clive Horrobin held a shotgun to his head.
1999 Forced into semi-retirement by ill health. Kept creeping back to work at Grey Gables until Caroline couldn't stand it and asked Peggy to restrain him.

What if...

Jack's heart were stronger. The Millennium Dome would have nothing on Jack's building schemes.

To everyone's relief Jack Woolley has handed over the day-to-day running of Grey Gables Hotel and Country Club to his efficient deputy, Caroline Pemberton. He had received several health warnings that he was working too hard and finally Peggy managed to persuade him to take things more easily.

Nevertheless, when he decided that Arkwright Hall, on the edge of his estate, was in need of restoration, he was there, putting life and limb in danger, before agreeing a long-term lease with the Landmark Trust.

Generous to a fault, and always the first to offer assistance to anyone in need, Jack at 81 is still a shrewd businessman at heart, and although at times he may appear naïve, it's hard to pull the wool over his eyes. Whether he can ever be persuaded to let go of the reins entirely and lead a quieter life in Ambridge with his beloved Peggy, remains to be seen.

It would be hard to think of Ambridge without Jack Woolley, Grey Gables and all that goes with it, and Jack would be the first to admit that Ambridge has become his spiritual home. After all, he did spend a great deal of his industrial fortune buying himself into a position in the village similar to that once held by Squire Lawson-Hope.

Grey Gables is now renowned throughout Borsetshire and beyond for all that it has to offer, from its famous French restaurant under Jean-Paul to the golf course, the country park with its lake, and the amalgamated shoot.

Although Jack is no longer the kingpin of the Village Council, he is still the proprietor of the local newspaper *The Borchester Echo*, giving him an unrivalled opportunity to express his views, which he does with great enthusiasm each week in The Proprietor's Column.

He is also the owner of that venerable establishment the Ambridge Village Shop and Post Office. Although Betty Tucker is given a free hand in running the shop there is no doubt that Jack uses it to find out what's going on in Ambridge, and if he takes a particular liking to a product then the shop stocks it.

It is hard to decide which has been the greater, Jack Woolley's influence on Ambridge, or the effect of the village on the former businessman from Stirchley. In 1961 he caused quite a stir when he arrived, determined to buy up everything in sight, knowing little and apparently caring less about life in the country.

What many would regard as the turning point in Jack's relationship with Ambridge was his marriage in 1991 to widow Peggy Archer. Since this, his third marriage, Jack has become more willing to delegate responsibility and consequently is enjoying life more. He even took an interest when a fashion show was staged at Grey Gables and, at great expense, bought his wife a most unsuitable dress.

It is also said that Jack is now resigned to not seeing or hearing from Hazel, his adopted daughter.

Arnold Peters

Born in London, Arnold has lived in Northamptonshire from an early age. After the RAF he joined Northampton Repertory Players and worked at the Royal Theatre there for five years.

His first broadcast was on the BBC's Children's Hour, then he joined the BBC Radio Repertory Company. He played Welsh shepherd Len Thomas and the Rev David Latimer in *The Archers* before taking over as Jack Woolley in 1980.

TV appearances include *Z Cars*, *The Onedin Line*, *Porridge* and *Citizen Smith*, and he toured 32 theatres playing Jack Woolley in *The Ambridge Pageant*.

He met his wife Beryl when they were in *Cinderella* in Northampton where she was a fairy and he was the Demon King. They have a daughter, Caroline, and two dance-mad granddaughters.

His hobbies include playing the drums in a folk dance band, and for whoever asks him to play.

Happy 10th birthday, Archers Addicts!

Archers Addicts is run by three musketeers – Hedli Niklaus (Kathy Perks), Trevor Harrison (Eddie Grundy) and Terry Molloy (Mike Tucker) – with a lot of help from cast and friends! Here, Hedli reviews some of the developments over the years. A lot of water has flowed under the bridge of the river Am since Archers Addicts was started in 1990...

We knew nothing and we had no equipment or office furniture. What we did have was a lot of goodwill. Cast members emerged from the studio to pack up envelopes with our first newsletters and a few goodies to those who had heard about us and wanted to become members. We learned how to manage VAT, understand business deals and create artwork – an art in itself. Now we have an office, computers, part-time staff and a flourishing website. It's an Ambridge story in its own right and, like *The Archers,* has a life of its own.

We learned two important facts. One that hardcore fans know more about Ambridge than we do. Secondly just how much the programme can mean to them. Fans make friends, run *Archers* discussion days and arrange gatherings for charity. The chat room on our website, www.archers-addicts.com attracts a lively group of fans who post pithy messages about the programme daily.

Archers Online – an everyday story of Chat-board addicts

Louise Bolotin, (on-line nickname LouBol) ,is one of the Chat-board's most prolific and outspoken contributors, and a regular at the Cyber Bull. She has been listening to *The Archers* on and off since the mid-1980s, mostly 'on' since she quit the UK to live in Europe and found it to be her most comforting link with home. She works as an editor for the publications department of a cultural foundation in the Netherlands and has

vowed to name her next cat Mrs A.

Here's what she has to say:

'Business is booming in the Cyber Bull these days. This virtual pub in cyberspace has become a home from home for hundreds of Archers Addicts who are also addicted to chatting on the official Addicts website. Sometimes Mike Tucker, Alistair Lloyd or David Archer have dropped in to the live chatroom to share a pint of Shires with the regulars. But mostly, we Cyber Archers use the message board to exchange our often heated views about what's happening in Ambridge.

'For example, Elizabeth Archer's tantrums over the family inheritance have firmly divided opinion as to whether she should get a slice of the Brookfield cake, while Debbie Aldridge's decision to try to take over Grange Farm when the Grundys faced eviction was roundly condemned and earned her an unprintable nickname! Debbie's choice of life partner also became rechristened as 'Slimon', demonstrating that no matter how hard he tries to ingratiate himself, he will never be accepted by anyone except the Aldridge women.

'Beyond that, we keep ourselves busy speculating on current plot lines, sometimes offering suggestions for future storylines, sometimes accurately predicting what will happen next week or the week after. And among the regulars, the in-jokes run thick and fast, such as the family of mallards behind a certain sofa ...

'Main moans: people typing in capital letters (all right, all right, no need to shout – we can all hear you!), anonymous lurkers

Hedli with Trevor and (below) Terry – the founding 'musketeers' of the Archers Addicts

(people who call in at the Cyber Bull but don't introduce themselves).

'Positive pleasures: sharing the highs and lows of Ambridge life with friends around the globe (yes, many friendships have been formed), knowing that Sid Perks understands the needs of his regular customers (another pint please, Sid), enjoying a daily belly laugh at other people's witty comments and perceptive insights (takes the tedium out of the daily grind at work).'

Addicts applaud!

In 1979 Richard Abraham was a policeman living with his fianceé in the police house, a perk of the job which meant that policemen could rent accommodation at an affordable rate. To his amusement his situation was mirrored in *The Archers* when young German au pair Eva Lenz got together with PC James Coverdale. Richard asked the actors (real-life married couple Leon Tanner and me, Hedli Niklaus) to his wedding. Many years later at the first Archers Addicts Convention at Pebble Mill in Birmingham, he was able to reassure them that his marriage was intact. No-one knows about James and Eva…

Richard says: 'The question most often asked of those of us who have been listening to *The Archers* for many years is: "Doesn't it spoil it for you knowing what they look like?" Given that "Radio has the best pictures" a lot of listeners much prefer to build their own images. In my case that is not so.

'Well before Ned Larkin opened my school fete in the early sixties and Walter Gabriel led the Weston-Super-Mare Dairy Festival 1970, I made a point of seeking out photographs of the cast, and so knowing exactly how they all looked. Then in 1990 came Archers Addicts, and my interest in meeting *The Archers* cast was made so much easier. If you imagine the very best kind of get-together with family and friends, then that is what you find an Addicts convention or other function is like.'

Richard Abraham – 'Knowing what the actors look like doesn't spoil the fun'

Archers Addicts **web words**

Adjuliate – coo and fuss over (especially male) babies, as long as they are clean and quiet.
Neil (verb) – what men are obliged to do when confronted by she-who-must-be-obeyed
Hayley (noun), the acme of perfection, recognisable by the "Haylo" above her head
Cursed tea – a dumped girlfriend, seemingly without good reason.
Brender – to turn speech into prose, usually in a professional capacity, for example on a newspaper or other media.
Clarrieluv (noun) A long-suffering, hard-working woman who shows unconditional devotion to her family, while said family constantly keep important things from her and are a complete waste of space.
(Not to be confused with a "clarrieluvell" – a female theatre impresario)
Edday (noun) – a person with poor financial skills
Wilyerm (noun) – small mammal given to skulking in woods and undergrowth, may bite if cornered or feels its family is endangered.

Fandom is fun!

Vicky Griffiths is a staunch supporter of Archers Addicts. She runs a penpal scheme and if you would like to know more about it you can contact her at Penfriends Unite, 18 Stoneleigh Gardens, Codsall, Staffs WV18 1AR.

'When I joined Archers Addicts I could never have foreseen the enjoyment and interest it would give, or the enthusiasm it would fire in me – fandom is fun!

'Conventions and events are a delight: the cast's friendliness, talks and entertainment and simply being with fellow Addicts mean a lot to me. I love the zany fantasy of it all. The quarterly issues of the club newsletter *The Ambridge Village Voice* with its news and features are another treat, as is the *Borchester Echo*'s whimsical look at Ambridge life.

'Archers Addicts brightens my life, despite ribbing from my family! And, like *The Archers,* it has me well and truly hooked.'

Magic moments

Organising events and creating memorabilia for Archers Addicts takes us to all sorts of fascinating places and enables us to meet some charmingly eccentric people.

A commemorative medal and suitably rural stamps for *The Archers* 50th anniversary in 2001 was a lovely idea but we needed the help of the Royal Mint and Royal Mail to turn it into a reality. When we heard the Curator of the Royal Mint, Graham

Vicky Griffiths – 'I love the zany fantasy of it all'

Dyer, is a follower of *The Archers* we knew we were home and dry! He invited us to spend a day at the Mint, where we saw how medallions are created from the design stage to the finished product. We actually ran our hands through hot freshly minted money – and were sad not to be allowed to take any away as a souvenir…

But the high spot was our session with Graham. He started collecting coins at age nine so being Curator at the Royal Mint is perfect casting! He showed us some of his special treasures – tissue-thin golden nobles which passed from household to household as a measure of status and were never used as common currency, and sample coins minted in advance of the reign of Edward VIII. Royal tradition is that the profile presented on coins alternates with each new sovereign but the much feted and adored Edward broke with tradition when, like any modern day film star, he insisted on presenting his 'best' profile.

Graham only has to hear the theme tune to be transported to his childhood. 'It was a family moment in the day when we would all cluster round the radio to find out what was going on in Ambridge,' he says.

He has a soft spot for Neil and is a bit worried about Shula. 'She used to be quirky but now she's conformist.'

Simon Drew

Simon studied biology at the University of Exeter, supports Friends of the Earth and named the business end of his enterprise, Plugprints, after his much-loved Collie. His drawings are crammed with lovingly detailed mammals, fish and birds. He has a quick eye for an artistic pun and a way with words that gives new meaning to the most innocent of phrases. You only have to think of Joined-up Whiting, or Cod Moving in Mysterious Ways! ('Biology is close to Art,' he told his professor a very long time ago. 'Nonsense!' came the reply. Simon is proud to have proved his point.)

We met Simon at the first *Country Living* Fair. To our great delight we discovered that he's listened to *The Archers*

Simon Drew – tributes to the characters

ROYAL MINT

for years and before we knew where we were he'd sketched out the design for a 'Fallen Archers' mug, featuring famous Ambridge partnerships Dan and Doris, Walter and Mrs P, and Jack Woolley's beloved Captain. Since then we've had 'Nelson's Swine Bar', 'I think therefore I Ambridge' and to celebrate the Addicts' tenth anniversary 'Signs of Ambridge'.

Graham Dyer – worried about Shula!

Addicts Memories

Highlights of Addicts events from the last ten years

Jack (Arnold Peters) calls for hush at the Barton Hall extravaganza in June 1999

Brenda (Amy Shindler) greets punters at the Addicts 10th anniversary convention at the Peacock Theatre, London in March 2000

Top: David (Tim Bentinck) raps his woes at the Barton Hall extravaganza

Above: Lynda (Carole Boyd) meets her adoring public at the tenth anniversary convention

Thank you for coming! The crowd at the Addicts convention at Malvern in 1994

The Archers Editor Vanessa Whitburn at the tenth anniversary convention

The Carters display 'alternative talents' at Barton Hall

Wendy Richard entertains Brian (Charles Collingwood), Shula (Judy Bennett), Phil (Norman Painting) in The Bull at an Addicts Out and About day

Guest star antiques expert Henry Sandon finds his way to the tenth anniversary convention and bumps into Hedli Niklaus

The ship Victoria which took Addicts on a P&O cruise to the Baltic capitals in 1999, and members of the cast on board. In 2000, the Archers Addicts took a Fred Olsen cruise to Scandinavia

Farmers' Market (with thanks to Colin Shaw) – just like the one in Borchester! Kathy (Hedli Niklaus), Pat (Patricia Gallimore) and Eddie (Trevor Harrison) are guests of honour at the first of three trial Farmers' Markets in Stratford upon Avon, Warwickshire

Mugs designed by Simon Drew for the Addicts

Eddie (Trevor Harrison) asks Jean-Paul (Yves Aubert) for tomato ketchup at Barton Hall

Lilian – the femme fatale

Echo reporter Betty Smith catches up with wealthy Ambridge ex-pat Lilian Bellamy, wild woman of the Archer clan, at her luxury home on Guernsey

From what I heard about Lilian Bellamy she could give me some tips on how to handle my own mid-life crisis. To find out more about her I chatted to her friends and family and it soon became obvious that I would have to meet the lady for myself at home in Guernsey. And what a lady! I wasn't there for five minutes before I found myself relaxing by the pool in the sun, sipping a (very potent) ice-cold sangria and being royally entertained by Lilian. This is her story.

'AMBRIDGE? FAR TOO SMALL FOR ME!'

Once upon a time there was a little girl called Lilian Archer. She lived in a village called Ambridge, which nestled in the heart of Borsetshire.

Lilian had an older sister called Jennifer and a younger brother called Tony. Her mother and father worked in The Bull.

'When I came home from school I'd often find Dad asleep on the sofa and Mum in a tight-lipped rage poring over the accounts,' Lilian recalls. 'They were always rowing but I didn't care. I'd be off to the stables and go for a ride and forget all about them.'

Lilian's passion was horses and she dreamed of the days when she would leave Ambridge and become Champion Horsewoman of the Year. 'I've always thought big and Ambridge was far too small for me!'

'LESTER NICHOLSON ABSOLUTELY GORGEOUS'

Then, at just 21, she fell in love.

'He was a pilot officer in the Royal Canadian Air Force, Lester Nicholson. Absolutely gorgeous – we met at the riding stables, of course.'

As if in a dream, Lilian married him and flew out with him to Canada. Only a year later she was to return to Ambridge, a forlorn young widow. Lester had died in hospital after a tragic fall.

'It seemed like the end of the world then, of course. We were very young. But life goes on and after Ralph and I got together I didn't have time to think of anything else much.'

'FATAL ATTRACTION'

Ralph Bellamy owned the Bellamy Estate and by all accounts had more money than he knew what to do with. Ruthless, powerful and rich he was 22 years older than Lilian. 'Oh, yes the fatal attraction of the older man. I could write a book! When he set his sights on me I didn't really stand a chance.'

Dazzled by his magnetism and authority, Lilian ignored all the advice of family and friends and married him.

'I've never let anyone tell me what to do. That was one of the main problems with Ralph. I thought he was romantic and masterful but looking back I reckon he was a bit of a bully.'

'MONEY BUYS A HELL OF A LOT OF COMPENSATIONS'

After the birth of their son, James Rodney Dominic, Ralph became increasingly autocratic, telling his wife to stop working at the stables and look after James. In 1976 his lifestyle took its toll on his heart and he decided to give up the stress of managing the Bellamy Estate. He moved his family to a big house in Guernsey.

'It was a living hell. There was nothing to do but drink and fight, and we did plenty of both. Poor old James just had to put up with it – I'm not what you would call a natural mother.'

It all proved too much for Ralph, who had a massive heart attack and died in 1980, leaving Lilian the entire Bellamy Estate. For a second time Lilian was faced with the loss of a husband, but this time she was a very rich woman.

'They tell you money doesn't buy you happiness but I tell you what – it buys a hell of a lot of compensations!'

'I HATE ALL THAT ANALYSIS STUFF'

It took her ten years to decide to sever all of her links with Ambridge and sell the Bellamy Estate and she spent the following ten years living a life of luxurious idleness. Her family has had to visit her at her island retreat if they wanted to see her and her appearances in Ambridge have been rare.

Might she come back to her home village one of these days?

'Who knows? I might enjoy a trip back, even if it's only to put the wind up a few of my stick-in-the-mud relatives. I hear they've got some new people since I was there last which might prove entertaining, especially if there's a gorgeous chap or two among them.

'But really I haven't a clue what I want – never have, apart from horses and I've missed the boat there. I hate all that analysis stuff about mid-life crisis or 'returning to your roots' kind of thing. Give me a stiff drink, and a good man – not necessarily in that order – and I'm okay.'

So no-one really knows what Lilian is looking for, least of all her. Ambridge wouldn't know what to make of Lilian, drinking, smoking, flaunting her short skirts and furs. But I bet if she did come back she'd ruffle a few feathers!

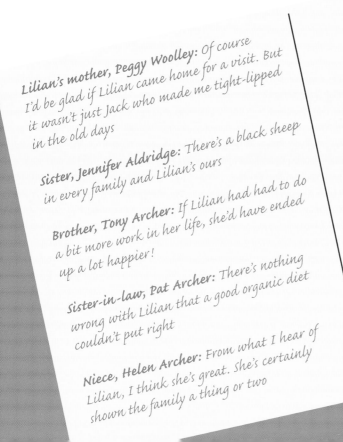

Lilian's mother, Peggy Woolley: Of course I'd be glad if Lilian came home for a visit. But it wasn't just Jack who made me tight-lipped in the old days

Sister, Jennifer Aldridge: There's a black sheep in every family and Lilian's ours

Brother, Tony Archer: If Lilian had had to do a bit more work in her life, she'd have ended up a lot happier!

Sister-in-law, Pat Archer: There's nothing wrong with Lilian that a good organic diet couldn't put right

Niece, Helen Archer: From what I hear of Lilian, I think she's great. She's certainly shown the family a thing or two

ISLAND OF GUERNSEY

26

village of Ambridge

The write stuff

...AND NOW ON RADIO 4 IT'S TIME FOR 'THE ARCHERS' AND OVER AT BROOKFIELD, JILL IS MAKING A CUP OF TEA...

'For the first time in her life Jill Archer has a problem with reality'

Peter Kerry does pictures as well as words. This is one of his series of surreal Archers cartoons.

Whether it's teen rebellion or death in the kitchen he's plotting, the life of *Archers* writer Peter Kerry is solitary but never dull

Writer **Peter Kerry** has had a hand in the decline of at least two elderly men in *The Archers*, so Phil, Jack, George and any other male of pensionable age will understandably worry if they see his name against their next storyline. In 1996, he was responsible for the death of Guy Pemberton and has recently contributed to the breakdown of Joe Grundy's health. Killing Guy, Caroline's distinguished if weak-hearted husband, was a real pleasure.

Peter says: 'I didn't want him to die nobly but to fall over and smash china, and I wanted to avoid the obvious drama of attempts at revival and the checking for pulse, like you get on *ER*. In the end I worked it so that Dr Richard Locke arrived too late to help and because Guy had fallen against the door, only Richard could get to him, leaving Caroline outside to worry.

'When she did get in, she had to wade through broken crockery to get to her husband's dead body. That was all juxtaposed with Lynda Snell trying to measure traffic speed through the village.'

Joe Grundy's depression has brought more meaty fare. 'I enjoy writing for several of the characters, including Lynda, Phil and Jill, David and Ruth, and the rest of the Grundys, but the easiest to write is Joe. I don't know why because I'm hardly an elderly working-class farmer from the West Midlands but I feel I relate to him best. If you're not careful, you can really overdo the Biblical quotes with Joe and make it very dark but the trick with all the Grundys is not to make them too cartoony because they then cease to be funny and so cease to be real.'

Peter joined *The Archers* writers six years ago with TV experience, particularly in children's drama, under his belt. A former actor, he first heard the programme while unemployed in the Eighties and has listened ever since.

'I was an actor but I didn't work very often. I was the king of "rest", in fact. I lived in a bedsit and couldn't afford a TV at the time so I started listening to the radio and caught the Omnibus edition of *The Archers* one weekend. Next week I found myself wondering what happened about that pig... Back then, I remember thinking that they were a fairly disagreeable lot. They have been warmed up and I think it works better that way.'

After three attempts at a trial script, he got on the writing team in 1994 and is now one of nine regular writers. After monthly script meetings, a writer produces a synopsis then has 11 days to write a week's worth of episodes. After second drafts and final editing, the whole process takes around three weeks. The story process is collaborative with everyone pitching in ideas but script-writing is a solitary task with hours spent honing and rewriting to produce the perfect Joe-like oath or plot twist.

It's dangerously easy for soaps to become trapped in their own legend, never evolving for fear of losing what originally made them popular. *The Archers* has avoided that trap, Peter believes, with its ability to move with the times. Its status as an institution, up there alongside the Cup Final and the Queen Mother as a totem of Britishness, could have proved a burden for a writer but the trick is to keep it relevant without jeopardising its traditions.

Peter says: 'I think people who pontificate about soaps are generally those who don't watch or listen to them. *The Archers* has lasted because it changes. It's always been right for its time. It's very successful now because it's tried hard to concentrate on the reality of the countryside today and that's right for now because people want to see their own lives reflected.

'In the Eighties, when people were more into froth and frivolity, it was more of a social comedy.

'As a writer, you're a custodian of *The Archers* but you don't want to keep it in aspic as a museum piece. The Grundys being thrown out was the sort of thing we should be doing as it's the reality of the countryside. To keep them on as a quaint little outfit of scallies who managed to survive on the dairy set-up they had would have been unrealistic.'

The next generation of Grundys has provided Peter and the rest of the writing team with a new writing challenge in the last 12 months, as Edward and his pal Emma Carter prepare to inherit the mantle of teenage rebels once held by the likes of Jennifer and Elizabeth. He wrote their first scenes which found them hanging out in the churchyard and Edward indulging in a spot of foolhardy steeple climbing.

Peter says: 'I loved writing them, though it's not because I consider myself terribly au fait with young people. There was a golden age a few years ago when our brat pack of Roy, Hayley, John and Kate were all teenagers. That was great but then they grew up and are now settling down, as young people are wont to do. I'm hoping that Edward and Emma will provide what we have lost there.'

'I found myself wondering what happened about that pig...'

Pitter Patter of Tiny Feet

Laura Polis who plays Phoebe

Never work with children or animals, goes the old showbiz adage. While the cast of The Archers are accustomed to competing with the odd baa, moo or grunt, children have gone relatively unheard with just the occasional crying babe to contend with. But listening parents know that, nowadays, children are definitely seen and heard, so more children's voices have been introduced to portray a more realistic picture of family life

The carefully chosen child actor is coached to get timing, intonation and inflexion right for each speech. Because this takes time, a special recording session is arranged in advance, using areas of the *Archers* studio in which the actual scenes will be recorded. Then the lines are played in for the adult actors to react to.

It demands skill and patience on the part of the production staff and the actors involved in the studio, sympathy from the child's parents, and a keen understanding of what is required from the child.

Here are some of the younger performers who have been making their contribution to *The Archers* in the past year:

HELEN PALMER - Pip Archer

Helen Palmer has played Philippa Rose Archer, daughter of Ruth and David Archer, since she was 16 months old. Helen is now seven like Pip. Her mother, Morag, says that generally she is rather a shy girl. Her first scripted words were 'sheep' and 'daddy', but she's come on well since then and shared animated scenes with grandma Jill Archer at the brilliant birthday party she organised. Jill even managed to bake a Princess in a Castle Cake, which Pip and all the girls loved.

Helen and her mum live in Bournville, Birmingham, so they can easily come to the studio to record Pip's lines with programme assistant Sonja Cooper.

DOMINIC DAVIES - Daniel Lloyd

Dominic is probably the most famous of the child voices heard in the programme. He plays Daniel Lloyd, (known to the cast as Two Dad Dan), Shula's son by Mark Hebden who was killed in a car crash. His stepfather Alistair Lloyd has now adopted him. There have been numerous storylines written specially for him, such as keeping the baby hedgehogs alive, the antics of Harry the Hamster, My Dad Alistair and The Wonder of Stag Beetles.

Daniel has had more to say than the other children in Ambridge, and Dominic Davies has been playing the role since he was 18 months old. His mother, Carol, has coached him in his performance. The writers heard the scenes with Daniel work well, which encouraged them to write more.

Credit must go to Judy Bennett who plays his mother Shula, and Michael Lumsden as new dad Alistair. They must interact with Dominic's lines, making it sound as if he is actually there with them.

Dominic has been a good mimic ever since he could talk. Now he's confident enough in the part of Daniel to comment sometimes: 'I don't think Daniel would say that'.

Just like Daniel, Dominic gets on well with animals. He enjoyed the stag beetles, which Daniel found in a tree

Graham Seed and Alison Dowling (Nigel and Lizzie Pargetter) with twins Lily and Freddie; Benjamin Minchin (Josh); Helen Palmer (Pip); Dominic Davies (Dani

stump next to his father Mark's grave in St Stephen's churchyard. Alistair told Daniel that they're very rare and brought home some leaflets from the surgery. When Daniel and Alistair were rearing the baby hedgehogs, Dominic was given a toy hedgehog to work with.

Almost six years old, Dominic has done voice-overs for the children's ITV series *Mopatop's Shop* and could have a long career in show business ahead of him.

LILY AND FREDDIE PARGETTER

Screams, cries and gurgles of the Pargetter twins are taken from stock sound discs in the BBC library. This picture (above) from *Radio Times* shows Nigel and Elizabeth each holding a baby. The 'twin' to the right is the younger child of actress Alison Dowling who plays Lizzie, while the baby on the left belongs to a friend of Alison. This picture was taken before Lily and Freddie were born!

LAURA POLIS – Phoebe Aldridge

Laura made her debut at just ten days old when she was pictured with Kate Aldridge (Kellie Bright) outside the Glastonbury tepee in 1998. *Archers* press officer Sandie Jefford was the one who found 'baby Aldridge' when the *Archers* team were on the look-out for a newborn to play the role. A friend who taught ante natal classes put her in touch with Laura's mother, Pam.

Laura was called again last autumn when scenes demanded words from Phoebe. She chats a lot and is persuaded to say the right words by her mum, usually

after a session playing with her toys and the microphone. She only has difficulty if she doesn't know the words – 'yo-yo' was tricky, Pam recalls.

When Laura hears the *Barwick Green* signature tune she pipes up, 'I'm going to be baby Phoebe'. Pam is taping her daughter's performances so that Laura can enjoy them when she's older (and get embarrassed when they're played to boyfriends). Laura had great fun in the pre-wedding scenes when Phoebe sat on Jennifer's hat, all but ruining it. She will continue to be heard with Roy and stand-in mother Hayley.

BENJAMIN MINCHIN – JOSh Archer

Two-year-old Benjamin was heard in great form on pancake day as Pip Archer's younger brother, Josh. His mother Caroline is a primary school teacher with two other small children, and she finds taking Ben to the studio most enjoyable. She says Ben is a sociable little boy who takes everything in his stride.

ALICE ALDRIDGE

Alice isn't heard at all at present, though we often hear about her. She certainly enjoyed being a ring bearer at her sister Debbie's wedding, especially as she was bought a beautiful dress for the occasion. Let's hope she'll find her voice before she gets too old!

The Archers 2051

How will Ambridge look in 2051?
Will Brookfield still be in Archer hands? Will the Bull still be serving Shires?
Let's take a peek at how the village might be as it celebrates its 100th anniversary...

Scientist Edward Grundy is knighted in King William's birthday honours. Sir Edward, who rose to fame in the early part of the century by isolating the snoring gene, dedicates the award to his late grandfather with the simple eulogy: 'He drove me to it.'

Phoebe Aldridge announces plans to expand her business empire. Thanks to the relaxation of restrictions on development in the green belt, Ms Aldridge, who has added 90 per cent of Borsetshire to the property portfolio bequeathed to her by her late grandfather, has been granted planning permission for 3,000 one-bedroom apartments in a series of condominiums on Lakey Hill. Local protests are led by her septuagenarian mother, Katherine, until she is promised one of the apartments rent-free.

Pip Archer is preparing for the latest round in her battle for ownership of Brookfield – or Bleak House as it has been nicknamed by locals. Ms Archer, who is contesting a claim by her cousins to a stake in her family home, said she would persevere with the legal fight, despite the mounting cost. Her cousins, living in a b&b in Felpersham, claim they are unable to use their own family home, Lower Loxley, as it is haunted by the ghost of a well-spoken lady of a certain age who constantly moves objects around, particularly money, and has been doing strange things to builders carrying out renovation work on the property. 'I never feel as if the place is my own,' complains Lily Pargetter.

At The Bull, the Speed Garage night introduced by landlady Fallon Rogers is going down well with the over 75s, although younger customers are complaining that the sight of OAPs out of their heads on Ecstasy and Sanatogen is interfering with their virtual dating. Ms Rogers inherited the pub from her mother whose memory is recalled in the stained glass window which dominates the entrance to the Ploughman's, portraying the late Jolene as Shania Twain.

Jamie Perks, captain of the Ambridge cricket team, says they need more players.

The funeral of Helen Archer takes place. Her obituary in the *Electronic Echo* recalls how the once dynamic businesswoman came to grief in the late Twenties when she attempted to expand the family chain of organic supermarkets just as organic produce was linked to a serious psychological disorder which turned sufferers into control freaks. Ms Archer spent the rest of her years working for family friend Hayley Tucker in a domestic capacity.

Daniel Lloyd, widower of the late Lilian Bellamy whom he married at age 16, allegedly causing the early demise of his mother through shock, has won a by-election. The new member for England South will take up his seat in Brussels shortly, where he is expected to campaign for farming to be reintroduced to the United Kingdom.

A pioneering medical technique enables Jack Woolley, cryogenically frozen back in 2010 at the grand old age of 91, to be revived. Thanks to a proviso in his will, Mr Woolley, now a youthful 132-year-old, is reinstalled as proprietor of Grey Gables, or GG as it was renamed in 2015. Locals swear the strange noise emanating from St Stephen's churchyard of an evening is the sound of Caroline Pemberton turning in her grave.

ARCHERS MUSEUM 2051

Brookfield Tapestry

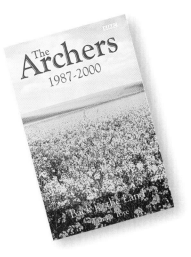

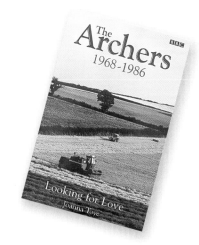

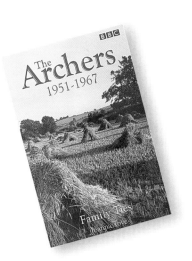

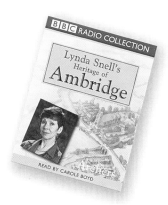

Archers Books and Audio Cassettes

Books

The Archers: The Ambridge Chronicles

A three-volume novelisation by Joanna Toye, telling the story of the Archers of Ambridge, starting in 1951, when the first programme was broadcast and taking the story right up to the 50th anniversary of *The Archers*, BBC Radio 4's favourite drama series.

The Archers 1951-1967
Family Ties

Introducing Dan, Doris, Phil, Christine, Jack and Peggy and their children.

The Archers 1968-1986
Looking for Love

Following the next generation of the Archers as they search for love and happiness in the changing world of the 1970s and 1980s.

The Archers 1987–2000
Back to the Land

Charts the progress of the Archer family as the younger generation grow up to face wider horizons than their grandparents ever imagined.

Who's Who in the Archers
Revised 2001

By Keri Davies
An A–Z pocket book listing the characters and places that appear in *The Archers* – the perfect guide for both newcomers and long-standing fans. Completely revised and updated.

Patricia Gallimore's Organic Year –
A Guide to Organic Living

An invaluable guide, *Organic Year* offers a comprehensive start-up guide to organic living.

Radio Collection

The Archers 1987–2000
Back to The Land

Read by Stephanie Cole
Four cassettes
Available 21 September 2000

Abridgements of the two other *Archers* novels by Joanna Toye are available on audio cassette:

The Archers 1951–1967
Family Ties

Read by Miriam Margolyes
Four cassettes

The Archers 1968–1986
Looking for Love

Read by Stella Gonet
Four cassettes

Other audio cassettes available from BBC Radio Collection:

Vintage Archers Volume One
Vintage Archers Volume Two
Vintage Archers Volume Three: The Lost Episodes
The Archers: The Third Generation
Lynda Snell's Heritage of Ambridge

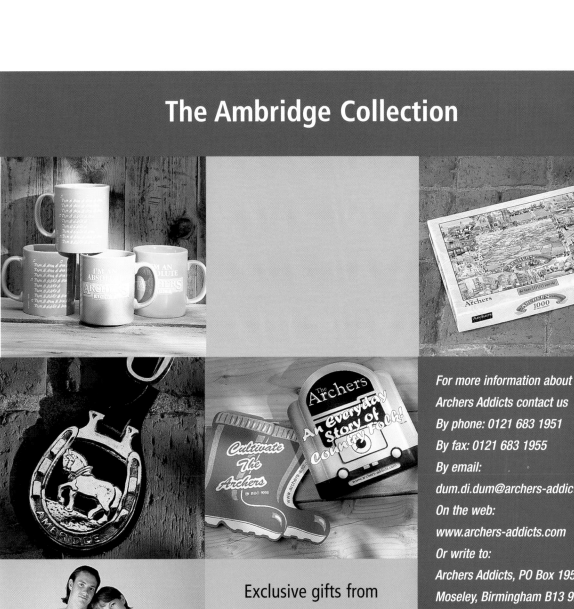

This book is published to accompany the BBC Radio 4 serial
The Archers
The Editor of *The Archers* is Vanessa Whitburn

Published by BBC Worldwide Limited, Woodlands, 80 Wood Lane,
London W12 0TT

First published 2000
Text copyright Kate Willmott with Hedli Niklaus 2000
The moral right of the authors has been asserted

All photographs copyright BBC except:
Pages 55–57 copyright *BBC Good Food* magazine, Anthony Blake
Photo Library;
Pages 23 (Bert Fry), 38–41 (The Bull, Jolene), 86 (Amy Shindler,
Carole Boyd, Vanessa Whitburn), 87 (Henry Sandon), copyright David
Willmott, (Victoria cruise), copyright Keri Davies
Cartoons pages 3, 16, 93 copyright Kipper Williams 2000
Map p12–13: design, Draughtsman Ltd; concept, Chris Moore

ISBN: 0 563 537167

Commissioning Editor: Emma Shackleton
Project Editor: Helena Caldon
Editor: Julie Nightingale
Art Direction: Linda Blakemore
Designer: Bobby Birchall, DW Design, London

Printed and bound in France by Imprimerie Pollina s. a. - n° L 80696
Colour separations by Imprimerie Pollina s. a.

Acknowledgements:
Our thanks to Helen Boaden, Controller of BBC Radio 4, for her kind
foreword, editor Vanessa Whitburn for her enthusiasm and
encouragement, senior producer Keri Davies for his input and advice
on the proofs, *The Archers* production team and scriptwriters, in
particular Peter Kerry, archivist Camilla Fisher and radio press officer
Sandie Jefford for their help in accessing BBC photographs, Julie
Nightingale for her patience and fortitude editing the annual, Bobby
Birchall and the DW team, Miriam Hyman at BBC Worldwide and Polly
Storr at Archers Addicts for their help with research, and Nicholas
Parsons for his fantasy storyline.
Thanks also to Mark Field for graphological help, Louise Bolotin,
Melissa Glenister, Maggie Eves, Morag Morrison for cyber-help, Vicky
Griffiths, Richard Abraham, Neville Withers for photographs, Lucy
Davis, Tim Bentinck, Arnold Peters and Trevor Harrison for their
contributions, Henry Sandon, Simon Drew and Graham Dyer.
Special thanks to David Willmott for all his help and support and for
his photographic input, and to Leon Tanner for his.

ANSWERS TO MIKE TUCKER'S QUIZ

The People Time's Forgot – One Pint Round

1. CLIVE HORROBIN
2. CAPTAIN
3. ALFRED – Alf for short.
4. PORTIA
5. HIGGS
6. MARTHA WOODFORD
7. MAUREEN TRAVIS – Mo
8. SHANE

Scored all eight? Yer a bloomin' marvel. Buy an extra pint – it's working.

The People Time's Forgot Quiz – Two Pints Round

9. BILL INSLEY
10. JASON THE BUILDER
11. ROSEMARY TARRANT
12. REV ROBIN STOKES
13. PADDY REDMOND
14. WALTER GABRIEL AND NED LARKIN
15. LEN THOMAS
16. VALERIE WOOLLEY before she married Jack she was Valerie Trentham.

**Scored 16? I'll go to the foot of our stairs. Are you a historian or summat?
I'll buy you a pint next time I see you.**

The People Time's Forgot Quiz – Three Pints Round

17. FREDA BANHAM....Not Elsie Catcher who was there for 16 years until she retired in 1967.
18. CORIANDER (known as Cas) and LEONIE (Len).
19. DOUGHY HOOD
20. MARY POUND
21. FLORRIE HOSKINS
22. TIM BEECHAM
23. DOLLY TREADGOLD
24. JOHN TREGORRAN

Scored 24. Yer a born milkman. Change jobs and come an' live in Ambridge.